CITYSPOTS
TURIN

Barbara Radcliffe R
& Stillman Rogers

Written by Barbara Radcliffe Rogers & Stillman Rogers
Updated by Kathryn Tomasetti

Published by Thomas Cook Publishing
A division of Thomas Cook Tour Operations Limited
Company registration No: 1450464 England
The Thomas Cook Business Park, 9 Coningsby Road
Peterborough PE3 8SB, United Kingdom
Email: sales@thomascook.com, Tel: +44 (0)1733 416477
www.thomascookpublishing.com

Produced by The Content Works Ltd
Aston Court, Kingsmead Business Park, Frederick Place
High Wycombe, Bucks HP11 1LA
www.thecontentworks.com

Series design based on an original concept by Studio 183 Limited

ISBN: 978-1-84157-877-4

First edition © 2006 Thomas Cook Publishing
This second edition © 2008 Thomas Cook Publishing
Text © Thomas Cook Publishing
Maps © Thomas Cook Publishing/PCGraphics (UK) Limited
Transport map © Communicarta Limited

Series Editor: Kelly Anne Pipes
Production/DTP: Steven Collins

Printed and bound in Spain by GraphyCems

Cover photography (Mole Antonelliana) © Giovanni Simeone/4Corners Images

CONTENTS

INTRODUCING TURIN

Introduction 6
When to go 8
Slow Food 12
History 14
Lifestyle 16
Culture 18

MAKING THE MOST OF TURIN

Shopping 22
Eating & drinking 24
Entertainment & nightlife 28
Sport & relaxation 30
Accommodation 32
The best of Turin 38
Suggested itineraries 40
Something for nothing 42
When it rains 44
On arrival 46

THE CITY OF TURIN

The Savoy centre 56
The Quadrilatero &
    Cittadella 72
Along the Po 94

OUT OF TOWN TRIPS

The Olympic mountain
    towns 116
Gran Paradiso &
    the Val d'Aosta 130

PRACTICAL INFORMATION

Directory 142
Emergencies 154

INDEX 156

MAPS

Turin city map 50
Turin transport map 53
The Savoy Centre 57
The Quadrilatero &
    Cittadella 73
Along the Po 95
The mountain towns,
    Gran Paradiso &
    the Val d'Aosta 118

SYMBOLS KEY

The following symbols are used throughout this book:

ⓐ address ⓣ telephone ⓕ fax ⓦ website address
ⓛ opening times ⓝ public transport connections ⓘ important

The following symbols are used on the maps:

ⓘ	information office	▪	points of interest
✈	airport	○	city
✚	hospital	○	large town
⛊	police station	○	small town
▣	bus station	═	motorway
▤	railway station	—	main road
Ⓜ	metro	—	minor road
✝	cathedral	—	railway
❶	numbers denote featured cafés & restaurants		

Hotels and restaurants are graded by approximate price as follows:

£ budget price ££ mid-range price £££ expensive

▶ *A bird's eye view of the city from Monte dei Cappucini*

Introduction

Turin comes as a surprise to those who don't know Italy – and even to those who think they do. No winding warrens of medieval streets (its 'medieval' quarter was built in the 1860s), no red sauce on the pasta (well, not very often), no long midday lull, no crying violins or tenors belting out *O Sole Mio*. Turin's favourite espresso is laced with chocolate (a civic passion) and its café scene is more like Vienna's than Florence's. This is not the Italy of Tuscan sun and coach tours.

This is the city where fast cars and Slow Food were born, where Michelangelo never set foot (Juvarra and Guarini are the names to know), where the *Risorgimento* (see page 15) is better known than the Renaissance, where Minis raced through the arcades and avenues in *The Italian Job*, and where the debated Holy Shroud and gay pride co-exist in relative peace.

Yet for all its differences, you would never mistake Turin for anything but intensely Italian. The daily *passeggiata* – early evening stroll – is alive and well, even in a city whose car manufacturing heritage leads to images of Detroit-on-the-Po. The Italian passion for food here takes the form of a reverence for fresh, locally produced ingredients, which include truffles, rice, delectable salamis and Barolo wine.

In place of winding cobbled streets, broad avenues spill out into elegant and graceful *piazze*, both lined by endless arched porticos. Although built in different eras and in somewhat different styles, these arcades give the city a satisfying harmony that ties together its exciting architectural past and future.

The names of architects seem to slip off the Turinese tongue with the same currency and respect as those of rock stars or football heroes, and once you've seen the dramatic works of Renzo Piano,

Mario Botta and their compatriots you'll understand why.
The startling transformation of the Lingotto building is a landmark
of contemporary design – inside and out.

And for every Old Master on the walls of its formidable number
of art museums and galleries you will see a dozen pieces of modern
art, from works of the greats – Paul Klee and Picasso – to those of
artists just hitting their stride and others on the cutting edge of
tomorrow's trends.

Turin revels in the unexpected, and despite its rich history
(or maybe because of it) takes pride in its edgy contemporary
outlook. This is Italy with attitude.

Piazza Castello is enchanting when night falls

When to go

SEASONS & CLIMATE

For the climate associated with sunny Italy, visit between April and October. Take an umbrella, but expect balmy days. These become even balmier in late July, and by August the heat is so oppressive that the city pretty much empties out, as locals decamp to the mountains or the sea. Although the mid-summer weather is definitely cooler in the nearby towns, hotels tend to be overflowing with city escapees. Between November and March, Turin is downright cold, with wind sweeping down from the Alps and a dense clammy fog settling in for a week at a time. Snow is not common in the city, falling instead on the mountain ski trails, often accumulating enough to make skiing possible through spring.

ANNUAL EVENTS

In addition to the following, Turin has been named the first World Design Capital for 2008, in honour of the city's slow and deliberate change from an industrial capital to an elegant European city. Throughout the year, the city will celebrate its status with events dedicated to contemporary design; for details, see Ⓦ www.torinoworlddesigncapital.it

February
Battaglia delle Arance (Battle of the Oranges) The three days before Ash Wednesday bring pageants, parades in medieval clothing and orange-throwing fights between neighbourhoods. ⓐ Ivrea (50 km (30 miles) north of Turin) Ⓦ news.carnevalediivrea.it

March
Automotoretrò A celebration of Italian automobile history at Lingotto Fiere. ⓐ Via Nizza 280 Ⓦ www.automotoretro.it

CioccolaTÒ A month of theatre, music, film, art and food – all celebrating chocolate. Ⓦ www.cioccola-to.com

April
Torino GLBT Film Festival (Turin International Gay & Lesbian Film Festival) Focused on films dealing with gay and lesbian issues. Ⓐ Corso Principe Oddone 3 Ⓣ 011 534 888 Ⓦ www.tglff.com
Il Gioco del Teatro A celebration of new theatre trends in Europe, with workshops and performances at Teatro Araldo, Teatro Garybaldi and Teatrino Civico. Ⓐ Casa del Teatro Ragazzi e Giovani, Corso Galileo Ferraris 266 Ⓣ 011 1974 0280 Ⓦ www.fondazionetrg.it

May
Fiera Internazionale del Libro Italian publishers and their books are the centrepiece of this annual book fair, with events for children and adults. Ⓐ Lingotto Fiere, Via Nizza 280 Ⓣ 011 518 4268 Ⓦ www.fieralibro.it

June
Documè in the Park Visit Parco del Valentino during June and July to view topical international documentaries, many of which focus on social and ethical issues. Ⓐ Parco del Valentino Ⓦ www.docume.org
Festivita Patronale di San Giovanni Battista (Feast of St John) On 24 June, Turin celebrates its patron saint, San Giovanni Battista, with processions, activities and a huge fireworks display.

July
Traffic Free Festival Top world bands and emerging local talent join in this annual festival of jazz, rock, techno and acid jazz. The concerts and performances are free, but entry is on a first-come, first-served basis at indoor events. Ⓣ 800 015 475 Ⓦ www.trafficfestival.com

International Guitar Festival Held at the Basilicata di Superga, this event encompasses a wide range of international styles.
🄰 Strada Basilicata di Superga 73 🄣 011 414 3231

September
Palio di Asti This horse race, preceded by a historical procession of people in medieval costumes, is the local version of the Palio race that has made Siena famous. Held on the third Sunday of the month.
🄰 Piazza Alfieri, Asti (45 km (28 miles) southeast of Turin)
🄦 www.palio.asti.it
Settembre Musica This prestigious classical music festival features top international musicians, with nods to avant-garde, contemporary, jazz and ethnic music. 🄦 www.settembremusica.it
Turin Marathon Run through the city and suburbs.
🄣 011 455 9959 🄦 www.turinmarathon.it

October
Fiera del Tartufo Bianco d'Alba Sampling and sales of the intensely flavourful white truffle, from October to early November.
🄰 Various locations, Alba (50 km (30 miles) southeast of Turin)
🄦 www.fieradeltartufo.org
Salone del Gusto (Taste Fair) Held in even years, this is one of the world's most popular food events. It's organised by the Slow Food movement (see pages 12–13), with producer displays, tasting and sales.
🄰 Lingotto Fiere, Via Nizza 280 🄦 www.salonedelgusto.it

November
Torino Film Festival In a city passionately devoted to film, the Film Festival focuses on international, emerging directors.
🄣 011 813 8811 🄦 www.torinofilmfest.org

Luci d'Artista An extravaganza of art in lights by international artists, this typically Turinese take on Christmas illuminations can be seen all over town from November to January.

Artissima (International Fair of Contemporary Art) Over 200 international galleries gather at the Lingotto complex for an exposition of contemporary art and a look at the newest art trends. 🅐 Lingotto Fiere, Via Nizza 280 Ⓦ www.artissima.it

December

Capodanno Turin's New Year's Eve festivities include an open-air concert in Piazza San Carlo; book early at restaurants.

Torino Anima Tango If you're a tango lover, don't miss this series of performances by some of the world's top dancers, held from late December to early January. 🅐 Aldobaraldo Via Parma 29 bis 🅣 011 242 2675 Ⓦ www.aldobaraldo.it

---

PUBLIC HOLIDAYS
New Year's Day 1 Jan
Epiphany 6 Jan
Easter Sunday 23 Mar 2008, 12 Apr 2009
Easter Monday 24 Mar 2008, 13 Apr 2009
Liberation Day 25 Apr
Labour Day 1 May
Republic Day 2 June
Patron Saint's Day 24 June
Feast of the Assumption 15 Aug
All Saints' Day 1 Nov
Christmas Day 25 Dec

Slow Food

It's a worrying fact that over the past 100 years more than 300,000 plants, including 30,000 vegetables, have become extinct. Fewer than 30 plants currently provide 95 per cent of the world's nutrition. It's statistics like these that have led an increasing number of people to question what we eat and how we grow and prepare it.

Carlo Petrini founded the Slow Food movement in 1989 in the town of Bra, just outside Turin. Arcigola, Slow Food's Italian forerunner, had been set up three years previously, just after the first McDonald's opened in Italy. Describing itself as 'the intersection of ethics and pleasure, of ecology and gastronomy', Slow Food actively campaigns against fast food, and 'fast life', which it claims is contemporary society's common error of mistaking speed for efficiency. It chooses instead to highlight the positive relationship between culture, sensual pleasure and the development of taste. Rather charmingly, the movement's mascot is a snail.

With more than 80,000 members around the world, Slow Food produces newsletters and books, and organises culinary workshops, fairs and events, each of which may focus on single ingredients or themes. One of these is the five-day Salone del Gusto, which is held every other year in Turin (even years) and draws in around 150,000 visitors. Small producers meet and exchange ideas, while visitors learn more about the processes and work behind the foods they purchase. Additionally, the Slow Food movement has opened the University of Gastronomic Sciences (www.unisg.it), with courses in Pollenzo (Piedmont) and Colorno (Emilia-Romagna), for those who are interested in pursuing careers in the world of ethical foods (classes are held in English and Italian).

If you're not in town for one of the Slow Food events, head out to **Eataly**, a massive food complex located on Turin's south side. Opened in 2007 in the former Carpano vermouth factory, the complex houses eight restaurants, two cafés, a gelateria, a library and a cooking school scattered within a giant indoor market. Slow Food runs workshops on a daily basis, focusing on everything from cheese to chocolate. (Workshops are primarily in Italian, call ahead for details.)
🅐 Via Nizza 230, Torino Lingotto ❶ 011 1950 6811 🅦 www.eatalytorino.it
🕙 10.00–22.00 Tues–Sun, closed Mon 🅝 Bus/Tram: 1, 18, 35

🔺 *Nibble your way through Slow Food's biennial Salone del Gusto*

History

The history of Turin – or at least that part of it that the casual visitor will meet – revolves around three factors: the Savoy family, FIAT and a succession of architects. Wrap these in the world's most famous shroud, and you've a bundle containing 90 per cent of historic references you will hear. The Savoys and FIAT each played lead parts in Italian history; most of the architects are not household names – with the possible exception of the brilliant contemporary, Renzo Piano.

In the dim beginnings, a tribe called Taurini formed the village of Taurisia, prospering quietly until Hannibal crossed the Alps with troops and elephants (without today's tunnels, most of these never made it over the frozen passes) in 218 BC.

Some 200 years later, Rome, on the make and moving north, rebuilt the settlement as Augusta Taurinorum, a few bits of which remain today. On the fall of Rome, the city's fortunes from the 4th century depended on which northern invader came through, until in 1046 the local countess married Count Odo of Savoy, beginning the rule of the Savoy family. By the 12th century the city was independent, making its living from tolls on highways and travellers.

The Savoys gradually extended their local holdings, rising to a duchy with their capital at Chambéry, France. Turin, meanwhile, grew rich enough to build a university in 1404. Spain and France fought over the region in the 15th and 16th centuries, but the Savoy dukes held on, finally moving their capital to Turin (bringing the Shroud with them). They rebuilt the city to rival the great capitals of Europe; today's city centre has changed little since that time.

The French again laid siege in 1706 but the Savoys won out in the Treaty of Utrecht, which gave them the title of ruling family. When Napoleon took a shine to Italy and controlled Turin, he left the

> ## RISORGIMENTO – BIRTH OF A MODERN NATION
>
> The *Risorgimento*, the revolutionary movement that lead to Italy's unification, spanned the period from 1815 to 1871. It began as Napoleon's reign ended and consisted of a complicated series of battles, rebellions and outright wars. The final result turned a group of disconnected and often warring states and cities into modern united Italy.

Savoys in charge. However, the winds of revolution were fanned by a group known as 'The Four Horsemen of the *Risorgimento*', stabled in Turin. The Savoyard King Vittorio Emanuele II wisely sided with these rebels, becoming king of the newly united Kingdom of Italy in 1861.

At the turn of the 20th century, the industrial age dawned with Olivetti and FIAT and a fast-growing film industry. In the economic depression of the 1930s, Mussolini's fascists helped Turin businesses put down problems with their workforces, setting the stage for later labour activism. When Italy switched allegiance from Hitler to the Allies in 1943, Germany occupied the city, whose factories were a target for heavy bombing. Continuing labour strife made Turin a popular base for the violent Red Brigades, whose murders and kidnappings captured the headlines in the 1970s.

In more recent times, the city again shifted economic footing as FIAT's fortunes changed; with the growth of mobile phones and wireless technologies, the whole region has become an important telecommunications centre. The sweeping modernisations that took place throughout the city in preparation for the 2006 Winter Olympics, combined with a growing reputation for food, wine and arts scenes, mean that Turin can now proudly boast tourism as one of its major assets.

Lifestyle

Despite its share of murky weather, Turin is an outdoor city, largely because of the 18 km (11 miles) of arcades that cover pavements and provide shelter for the myriad cafés. You could easily think that at any time of day at least half the population is taking an espresso break or getting a head start on the aperitif hour.

The Savoys, who enoyed their fair share of café life, also set the pattern for Turin's cultural climate, commissioning up-and-coming architects to design their new capital, building theatres and encouraging art and music in the fashion of the older courts of Europe.

After the royals came the automobile aristocracy, who may have set a different tone from the court's gaiety, but continued to support the cultural life of Turin. Although the Turinese may work hard, they play hard, too, and they play on the edge. The city's reputation as one of Europe's most avant-garde cities in terms of art and music began

● *Partake in Turin's preferred pastime – the early evening* aperitivo

a century ago with the newly affluent bourgeoisie, who built homes and even factories in the daring art nouveau style, and patronised contemporary artists, architects and designers to furnish them. Today it is the city's popular electronic music scene, as well as its stunning contemporary architecture, that keep it at the cutting edge.

While regarded as dour by southern Italians, industrial, hard-working Turin has been influenced by large numbers of Sicilian workers lured here from economically depressed villages by a steady income in the car factories. Its thanks to this group of 'immigrant workers' that Turin has so many pizza parlours, and thanks to the newer wave of foreign workers that the city enjoys an increasing number of ethnic restaurants.

Turin's university has always had a free-thinking influence on the city, attracting and nurturing political thinkers and activists. It is not surprising that the *Risorgimento* began here and succeeded, unifying the many fragmented little states that now make up the country.

Turin is without doubt a Catholic city – don't suggest too loudly that there is any uncertainty about the authenticity of the Holy Shroud – but it carries on the liberal traditions of its past, too. You will notice a live-and-let-live attitude here: Turin led Italy's emerging gay movement in the 1970s, and is arguably more welcoming to the openly gay and lesbian than any other Italian city. Along with gay nightspots, the city is home to **Circolo Maurice** (☎ 011 521 1116 Ⓦ www.mauriceglbt.org), a social and sports club that acts as a clearing house for gay, lesbian and transgender events and venues, and **Informagay** (☎ 011 851 743 Ⓦ www.informagay.it), a meeting place and information point for the gay and lesbian community.

Balancing their active cultural and social life, the Turinese enjoy sports, not only as spectators at Juventus and (in particular) Torino football matches, but with active individual sports as well.

Culture

The Savoy family established Turin's reputation as an arts capital. Much of its patrimony remains today, with entire museums, such as the Egyptian and the Museo di Antichità, filled with the treasures the family collected and passed on to the city.

The Savoys are not the only family that has shared its largesse with the public. More recently, the Agnelli family, of FIAT fortune, has opened an art exhibition space showing 25 paintings of their outstanding collection, and a palace full of decorative arts was donated to the city by an antiques dealer.

This tradition of patronising the arts extends to the general public as well. The Turinese are avid concert-, opera- and theatre-goers, and they honour the city's status as the birthplace of the Italian film industry with good first-run cinemas and a state-of-the-art cinema museum (see page 105).

In addition, Turin residents are frequent visitors to the art and design galleries sprinkled among the shops of the Quadrilatero, Citadella and along streets such as Via Mazzini. The Fondazione Italiana per la Fotografia is based in Turin, and the opening of its headquarters near Porta Palazzo in 2004 provided much-needed space for major exhibitions. Their projects include the prestigious Biennale Internazionale della Fotografia.

Large exhibition spaces are devoted to the paintings, sculpture and photography of contemporary artists, whose work is encouraged and valued. To learn what's happening in the smaller galleries and the alternative theatres and small venues, browse the walls and the cafés around the university, north of Via Po, or check with the tourist

▶ *Turin celebrates Italy's cinematic heritage at the Cinema Museum*

● *Art lovers – and collectors – are well catered for*

office on Piazza Solferino. *Torino Sette*, the Friday cultural supplement issued with Turin's daily newspaper, *La Stampa*, provides the most comprehensive weekly listings Ⓦ www.torinosette.it. Additionally, look for street stands stocking the free *News Spettacolo Torino* Ⓦ www.torinospettacoli.com. Its website carries complete information on performances, with ticket booking details and prices.

The very useful Ⓦ www.extratorino.it and the official tourism site Ⓦ www.turismotorino.org both have English versions with details on venues and tickets and links to individual venues. The tourism site also shows the current special exhibits and programmes at galleries and museums.

▶ *Eighteenth-century arcades in central Turin*

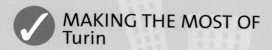

MAKING THE MOST OF
Turin

Shopping

It's been many years since Turin let its claim as Italy's fashion capital slip to the catwalks of Milan, but *la moda* is as important here as ever. The city still has its own designer fashion scene, and shopping – or at lease browsing in windows – is a national pastime.

Prices in the Hermès and Ferragamo emporia of Via Roma are high, but you can often find bargains on designer wear in outlet shops, such as Il Pallino (for shoes) and in the morning market in the streets around Largo Cassini. Along with Via Roma and Piazza San Carlo, Via Lagrange has a concentration of high-end shops. These and others in the main shopping streets are normally open from 09.00 or 10.00 until 19.00 or 19.30, with smaller shops closing for an hour or two at lunch.

For funkier clothing, try the boutiques under the arcades of Via Po and the shops lining a solid kilometre of Via Garibaldi. Via Mazzini has a bit of both worlds, with trendy shops – but not quite such rarefied price tags – and friendlier sales clerks. Across the river in Borgo Po, more highbrow boutiques satisfy the residents of the city's classiest neighbourhood.

The Piedmont is well known for its distinctive food and drink: Arborio rice from the Po valley, Borolo and aperitif wines, dried mushrooms, hand-rolled breadsticks and Turin chocolates are only a few of the delicacies travellers take home from this region.

Those who like their kitchens to be as fashionably dressed as themselves will love the variety and quality of culinary and table accessories. The whimsical and bright plastic accessories by Alessi are made nearby, so you can be sure of seeing their latest designs in Turin kitchenware shops.

Via Mercanti in the Quadrilatero is known for its fine craftsmen, and you can find hand-bound books and notebooks and fine letter

USEFUL SHOPPING PHRASES

What time do the shops open/close?
A che ora aprono/chiudono i negozi?
Ah keh ohrah ahprohnoh/kewdohnoh ee nehgotsee

How much is this?
Quanto costa questo?
Kwantoh kostah kwehstoh?

Can I try this on?
Posso provarlo?
Pohsoh prohvarloh?

My size is ...
La mia taglia è ...
Lah meeyah tahlyah eh ...

I'll take this one, thank you
Prenderò questo, grazie
Prehndehroh kwestoh, grahtsyeh

Can you show me the one in the window/this one?
Può mostrarmi quello in vetrina/questo?
Poh mohstrahrmee kwehloh een vehtreenah/kwehstoh?

This is too large/too small/too expensive
Questo è troppo grande/troppo piccolo/troppo caro
*Kwehstoh eh trohpoh grahndeh/trohpoh peekohloh/
trohpoh kahroh*

paper here. In nearby Piazza Solferino is a venerable shop specialising in hand-finished candles (Colenghi, see page 84). If you head out into the mountain towns to the west and north, look for typical alpine crafts, including excellent woodcarving.

Eating & drinking

Everyone knows about Italian food: delicious, plentiful and hearty. But first-time visitors to Turin and the Piedmont may be in for a surprise. This region has its own distinctive cuisine, very different from the traditions of southern Italy.

You're more likely to see cream-based sauces than tomato-based ones here, and risotto often wins out over pasta. Farm-fresh vegetables, mushrooms from the mountains, delicious local cheeses and trout are all products of the surrounding region. It was in the Piedmont that the Slow Food movement was born (see pages 12–13), and it continues to gather advocates who shun both fast foods and those made with out-of-season imported produce.

Food is a major part of the Italian experience, but it can be pricey. Like the best restaurants anywhere, those in Turin match their quality with high menu prices, although they are noticeably lower than in Rome, Venice or Florence.

One euro-stretching strategy is to shop in markets, such as the daily one in Porto Palazzo, for picnic ingredients (the local sausages, salami and breads are all excellent) and carry the results of your foraging to Giardini Reali, behind the palace, or to the riverside Parco del Valentino. To dine with a view, hop on a bus across the river and picnic on the terraces of one of the churches overlooking the city.

PRICE CATEGORIES

Restaurant ratings in this book indicate the average cost of a main dish, without drinks.

£ up to €10   **££** €10–€20   **£££** over €20

THE MENU

What should you order from the menu? First, remember that although it lists *primi* (first courses) and *secondi* (second courses) along with the *antipasti* (starters) and *dolci* (pudding), not all Italians order all four. No-one will think it odd if you choose fewer courses – even one, as long as it is one of the two mains. If you like vegetables, order them from the *contorni* (side dishes) list.

Local specialities include *bagna cauda*, raw vegetables dipped in a rich sauce of olive oil, garlic, anchovies and occasionally, cream. *Agnolotti*, a type of ravioli stuffed with different fillings, and *tajarin*, a deep yellow, thin-cut egg pasta, are local specialities. *Brasato al Barolo* is veal braised in Barolo wine and a *fritto misto* (mixed fried platter) here will be more meat than seafood. The region is renowned for its creamy *zabaglione*, *panna cotta* and for a chocolate and almond cake called *bonet*.

WINE WISE

Piedmont wines span the bounds of taste, from the fizzy party wine Asti Spumante to some of the finest Italy produces. Wine bars give you a chance to sample these by the glass without committing to a bottle. Look for the big bold Barbaresco, Barbera d'Alba and Barolo reds and Gavi or Roero Arneis whites. From the nearby vineyards of Lombardy come the dry red Botticino and Cellatica, and the softer and more floral Gropello.

PRACTICAL DETAILS

Turinese dine late by northern European standards, and many restaurants don't even open until 19.30 or 20.00. Lunch is served from 12.30 until 14.30 or 15.00. It's best to book ahead (or ask your hotel to), especially for popular restaurants on Friday and Saturday evenings.

The lines between *trattorie*, *osterie* and *ristoranti* are becoming more blurred. Originally an *osteria* was a tavern that sold simple meals of local origin, in a less-than-fancy setting. Today, some still follow traditional definitions, but you'll also come across very expensive 'country inn' dining spots that may call themselves *osterie* too, so you can't tell by the name.

Osterie and cafés usually stay open later than restaurants, which normally shut the kitchen at 23.00. Many restaurants close on Monday and Tuesday, and those travelling in mid-August may have trouble finding anywhere to eat in Turin; this period is when Italian city-dwellers generally go on holiday.

In most city restaurants you can pay by credit card, although smaller *osterie* and *trattorie* may accept only cash. Tipping, while

● *Turin blends traditional cuisine with edgy décor*

USEFUL PHRASES

I would like a table for ... people
Vorrei un tavolo per ... persone
Vohray oon tahvohloh pehr... pehrsohneh

May I have the bill, please?
Mi dà il conto, per favore?
Mee dah eel cohntoh perh fahvohreh?

Excuse me! Scusi! *Skoozhee!*

Could I have it well-cooked/medium/rare please?
Potrei averlo ben cotto/mediamente cotto/al sangue, per favore?
*Pohtray ahvehrloh behn kohtoh/mehdyahmehnteh kohtoh/
ahl sahngweh, pehr fahvohreh?*

I am a vegetarian. Does this contain meat?
Sono vegetariano/vegetariana (fem.). Contiene carne?
*Sohnoh vehjehtehrehahnoh/vehjehtehrehahnah.
Kontyehneh kahrneh?*

appreciated, is not a fixed amount. A ten per cent tip is considered lavish; €2–€5 is a respectable tip, depending on how fancy the restaurant is, and a 20-cent tip is adequate at a bar. Larger upmarket restaurants may add a service charge, which should be mentioned on the bill, and no further tip is expected.

Entertainment & nightlife

Turin's club culture is the most progressive in Italy, and among Europe's most active. Spurred on by the university population, the city's unusual scene centres around reggae, jazz and drum'n'bass, but includes just about every known style from Black (Doctor Sax) to teenage bopping (Tuesday at Scapadacà). The action begins late – not until midnight at most places – and the venue changes with the season. In the summer it's along the Po, at Murazzi, and when the weather turns, the scene moves inland to Docks Dora, northwest of the centre. Traditional discos and clubs in the Murazzi begin around midnight and are usually open until 04.00, with some in the Docks Dora staying open until 06.00 (and even longer on Sunday morning).

Since the blast of Xplosiva onto European consoles, Turin and the Piedmont region have been the focus of international attention for their contemporary electronic music. Dubbed the Piemonte Groove, the best-known artists include Turin-based Subsonica, Mau Mau, Africa Unite and Eiffel 65. Along with these attention-getters are even more underground and experimental groups and artists. Find out more about them and learn where you can dance to Piemonte rhythms at ⓦ www.piemontegroove.com

Many of the Docks Dora venues belong to ARCI and AICS, associations that require membership for entrance. You can buy this at the door, but it may not be worth it for a few nights. Plead your case as a stranger in town who's heard how great the Turin scene is, and they'll probably find a way to let you in. Take a spare ID (not your passport) that you can leave at the door – and don't forget to retrieve it. Bars always have free admission, even when there's live music. Nightclubs and discos usually charge €10–25, depending on who is playing and how prestigious the place considers itself.

Turin is a city of music festivals, the biggest of which is Traffic in July, which brings in top performers every year – including Aphex Twin, Lou Reed and Carmen Consoli – for free concerts. The list of live performance venues for rock concerts grew longer with the new stadiums built for the Winter Olympics, and now includes the Mazda Palace, the Ruffini, the Lingotto auditorium, the Rai and the hockey stadium.

With all the clubs and contemporary music on offer, it's easy to overlook Turin's long tradition of classical music, opera, ballet and theatre. **Teatro Stabile** is an umbrella organisation where you can get information and tickets for both classic and innovative performances staged at several theatres (ⓦ www.teatrostabiletorino.it). Teatro Regio is the place to seek opera, classical music and ballet. Dozens of other theatres showcase plays, comedies and cutting-edge performances (**Teatro Settimo** ⓐ Via Beccarla ⓣ 011 800 5550) is best known for these) and even marionette plays.

Turin is most closely associated with the cinema, as the birthplace of Italian motion pictures with the release of Pastone's *Cabiria* in 1914. New cinemas are opening and old ones have been modernised into high-tech, multi-screen complexes. Most impressive of these is the 11-screen Pathé Complex at the Lingotto. The Torino Film Festival in November continues the city's strong tradition of art films, and an entire museum is devoted to world cinema.

La Stampa lists performances with ticket information daily, but the best source is its weekly *Torino Sette*, published every Friday with complete listings ⓦ www.torinosette.it. The Italian website ⓦ www.torinospettacoli.com has the latest updates on performances, tickets and prices. *News Spettacolo Torino* is available free from street stands, with performance listings and information on clubs and bars.

Sport & relaxation

The 2006 Winter Olympics have made this sports-crazy city even more passionate about their favourite pastimes. Over three-quarters of the native population skis, 100 km (60 miles) of cycling paths criss-cross the city, and the first thing you will learn about a new acquaintance is their favourite football team – be it Juventus or Torino.

Paddle boats and rowing teams use the river, Parco del Valentino is filled with weekend joggers, and bicycles are used more for recreation than transportation. With world-class skiing less than an hour from the heart of the city, snow sports are so popular that schools close for *settimana bianca* ('white week') in February so that families can enjoy them together.

Runners and joggers will find lots of company in any of the city's parks, especially Parco del Valentino, along the river, where the shaded paths are shared with walkers. But the best only-in-Turin running experience is on La Pista, the former FIAT test track on the roof of the Lingotto factory. The track is free to guests of the Meridien hotel – just ask at reception for a key, then take the lift for the art gallery and go through the glass doors to find 1.1 km (0.7 miles) of running surface. Every April Turin also hosts one of Italy's top marathons (**t** 011 455 9959 **w** www.turinmarathon.it).

The unloved Stadio delle Alpi (**a** Viale Grande Torino **t** 011 739 5759), home of Juventus and Torino, is rarely filled except for games against Milan, Italian Cup or other title games. Buy tickets at the stadium or at the team stores: **Juventus a** Via Garibaldi 4 **t** 011 433 8709 **w** www.juventustore.com; **Torino a** Piazza Castello 10 **t** 011 542 348 **w** www.torinofc.it. You will need photo ID when you buy the tickets, and you must take your ID and tickets to the game.

Outdoor swimming pools open to the public include **Lido Torino** (🄰 Via Villa Glori 21 🄣 011 661 4888) and **Pellerina Estiva** (🄰 Corso Appio Claudio 110 🄣 011 744 036). An enclosed pool is at **Sebastopoli** (🄰 Corso Sebastopoli 260 🄣 011 335 437). Keep up your training regimen, where there are weights and gym equipment, at **Playtime** (🄰 Via Lagrange 27 🄣 011 562 0520).

On good weather weekends you can hire bicycles at impromptu stands at major parks, including **Valentino** (🄰 Viale Ceppi) and **Colletta** (🄰 Via Carcano), as well as at the Atrium in Piazza Solferino. You can begin at Colletta, on the city's north end, and cycle along the river and all the way to Stupinigi Palace and park to the south. You can download a map of the city's cycle paths at 🅦 www.comune.torino.it/ambiente/bici/piste-bici.pdf

◆ *Cycle to the stunning Stupinigi Palace*

Accommodation

Hotels, ranging from cheerfully homely to state-of-the-art Euro-modern, are conveniently scattered throughout the city, with some of the least expensive in the most convenient locations. Don't be surprised to find well-kept family-run hotels occupying the top floor of a fine old building, perhaps once a *palazzo* belonging to lesser members of the Savoy court. Breakfast is often included, and may be anything from a couple of bread rolls and a cup of coffee to an elegant buffet spread, such as the one at Hotel Victoria. Booking ahead will not only save you time on the ground but will also mean you can find the best deals. Conventions can spontaneously fill the city, making rooms scarce – another reason to book ahead. Tip: many hotels discount their rates at the weekend, and/or offer a 'Week-end a Torino' package, including two nights' (heavily discounted) accommodation, and a 48-hour Torino Card (see page 52) per person. Check with the tourist office for a full list of participating hotels. For assistance with last-minute lodging, head to the friendly information office in Atrium Torino, at Piazza Solferino.

Turin is small and compact enough that virtually all the following hotels are convenient to the sights.

HOTELS

Art'Tò B&B £ If art's your passion, pick this place, which features a beautiful selection of paintings by local artist Valerio Capra, as well as an abundant and fresh breakfast. A unique find. ⓐ Corso Duca degli Abruzzi ⓣ 393 915 0111 ⓦ www.art-to.it ⓝ Bus: 10, 12

Due Mondi £–££ Decorated in bright and attractive colours, this small hotel is close to the city centre. Most rooms have internet. ⓐ Via

Saluzzo 3 ☎ 011 650 5084 🖷 011 669 9383 ⓦ www.hotelduemondi.it
Ⓝ Bus/Tram: 9, 18, 34, 35, 52, 61, 67, 68

Hotel Artua & Solferino £–££ Just a short walk from the shops on Via
Roma, this family-run hotel is a welcoming blend of hotel and hostel,
with a guest kitchen, in-room internet access, private baths, all on the
top floor of a fine 19th-century building. ⓐ Via Brofferio 3 ☎ 011 517 5301
🖷 011 562 2241 ⓦ www.hotelartuasolferino.it Ⓝ Bus/Tram: 5, 14

Hotel Principi d'Acaja £–££ Set in a gorgeous early 20th-century family
home, this hotel may be basic, but it oozes character. One of the city's
friendliest budget options, and just a five-minute walk from the Porta
Susa train station. ⓐ Via Principi d'Acaja 8 ☎ 011 433 8348 🖷 011 430 4610
ⓦ www.hotelprincipidacaja.com Ⓝ Bus/Tram: 9, 65, 68

Conte Biancamano ££ With only 24 rooms, staying at this
family-run hotel in the middle of town is like visiting friends.
ⓐ Corso Vittorio Emanuele II 73 ☎ 011 562 3281 🖷 011 562 3789
ⓦ www.hotelcontebiancamano.it Ⓝ Bus/Tram: 9, 18, 34, 35, 52, 61, 67, 68

Hotel Alexandra ££ Although located slightly out of the city centre,
this small hotel boasts newly revamped family suites, which offer

great value for three or more people.  Lungo Dora Napoli 14
 011 858 327  011 248 3805  www.hotel-alexandra.it  Bus: 10, 11

Hotel Amadeus ££ Perfectly positioned just off the bustling Via Po,
the Hotel Amadeus offers guests simple accommodation in a beautiful
Stile Liberty (art nouveau) building.  Via Principe Amadeo 41 bis
 011 817 4951  011 817 4953  www.hotelamadeustorino.it
 Bus/Tram: 11, 12, 27, 58, 61, 68

Hotel Chelsea ££ This small, conveniently located hotel (near the
Duomo) has been newly renovated and modernised. Rates are lower
on weekends.  Via XX Settembre 79/E  011 436 0100  011 436 3141
 www.hotelchelsea.it  Bus/Tram: 4, 11, 12

NH Santo Stefano ££ Blending top-end business facilities with
minimalist design, the huge Santo Stefano is just around the
corner from Piazza Castello. Spacious and simple, it's a good base
for a work trip.  Via Porta Palatina 19  011 522 3311  011 522 3313
 www.nh-hotels.com  Bus/Tram: 4, 11, 12, 57

Piemontese ££ You get a friendly welcome at this extraordinary
art nouveau mansion. Top-notch modern amenities include private
Jacuzzis and high-speed internet.  Via Berthollet 21  011 669 8101
 011 669 0571  www.hotelpiemontese.it  Bus/Tram: 34, 52, 67, 68

Art Hotel Boston ££–£££ One of the most interesting hotels in Turin,
the Boston's rooms toe the line between sumptuous and over the
top, each one featuring fabulous original works by one of around
40 contemporary artists.  Via Massena 70 / 011 500 359
 www.hotelbostontorino.it  Bus/Tram: 4, 12, 63

Many of the hotels are right on the spot for sightseeing

Best Western Hotel Genio ££–£££ Situated next to the Porta Nuova rail station, this hotel has retained vintage details, while adding modern creature comforts such as Wi-Fi access. ⓐ Corso Vittorio Emanuele II 47 ⓣ 011 650 5771 ⓕ 011 650 8264 ⓦ www.hotelgenio.it ⓝ Bus/Tram: 9, 18, 34, 35, 52, 61, 67, 68

Le Meridien Lingotto ££–£££ Designed and converted under the direction of Renzo Piano, Lingotto has retained original features, such as the glass walls, from its previous incarnation as the FIAT automobile factory. The former car test track is on its roof, where you can admire breathtaking views of the Alps. ⓐ Lingotto complex, Via Nizza 262 ⓣ 011 664 2000 ⓕ 011 664 2001 ⓦ www.lemeridien-lingotto.it ⓝ Bus/Tram: 1, 4, 35

Starhotels Majestic ££–£££ Well located opposite Porta Nuova station, the Majestic has been renovated to its original 19th-century style. Modern touches include Wi-Fi accessibility. ⓐ Corso Vittorio Emanuele II 54 ⓣ 011 539 153 ⓕ 011 534 963 ⓦ www.starhotels.com ⓝ Bus/Tram: 9, 18, 34, 35, 52, 61, 67, 68

Golden Palace £££ This new 5-star hotel is luxury all the way, with rooms decorated in sophisticated colour schemes. Don't miss the on-site spa facilities, including Turkish bath and swimming pool (although note that they're closed for the summer holidays). ⓐ Via Arcivescovado 18 ⓣ 011 551 2111 ⓕ 011 551 2880 ⓦ www.thi.it ⓝ Bus/Tram: 29, 65

Grand Hotel Sitea £££ A beautifully renovated classic hotel with abundant amenities, just off Piazza San Carlo. The elegant atmosphere creates an ideal ambience for business or a weekend break. ⓐ Via Carlo Alberto 35 ⓣ 011 517 0171 ⓕ 011 548 090 ⓦ www.thi.it ⓝ Bus/Tram: 11, 27, 57, 63, 65, 72

Le Meridien Art+Tech £££ Strikingly modern, the Renzo Piano-designed Le Meridien Art+Tech does as its name implies, combining the best of contemporary art styles and the latest technology. ⓐ Lingotto complex, Via Nizza 230 ⓣ 011 664 2000 ⓕ 011 664 2004 ⓦ www.lemeridien-lingotto.it Ⓝ Bus/Tram: 1, 4, 35

Town House 70 £££ Boutique chic in a 19th-century package, the Townhouse 70 is Turin's coolest new arrival. Rooms are decked out with cutting-edge designs, and staff are charmingly efficient. ⓐ Via XX Settembre 70 ⓣ 011 1970 0003 ⓕ 011 1970 0188 ⓦ www.townhouse.it Ⓝ Bus/Tram: 4, 11, 12

Victoria Hotel £££ Right in the heart of Turin's historical centre, yet with the elegance and feel of a country house, the Victoria is an ideal choice for a pampering city break. Each room is uniquely furnished, and guests have the use of free internet and bicycles. An on-site pool and spa are further draws. ⓐ Via Nino Costa 4 ⓣ 011 561 1909 ⓕ 011 561 1806 ⓦ www.hotelvictoria-torino.com Ⓝ Bus/Tram: 1, 56, 65

B&BS & HOSTELS
Bed & Breakfast Aprile ££ Located in the trendy Quadrilatero area, this little B&B comes with private bathrooms, organic cotton mattresses – and rooftop sunsets. Choose one of three unique rooms, or two beautifully renovated lofts. ⓐ Via delle Orfane 19 ⓣ 011 436 0114 ⓦ www.aprile.to.it Ⓝ Bus: 3, 16, 52, 60

Ostello per la Gioventù Torino £ Across the river on a hillside with views over the city, the hostel offers canoe and kayak classes, as well as Wi-Fi throughout. ⓐ Via Alby 1 ⓣ 011 660 2939 ⓕ 011 660 4445 Ⓝ Bus: 52, 64

THE BEST OF TURIN

Whether you're on a flying visit to Turin or taking a more leisurely break in northern Italy, the city and its surroundings offer some sights, places and experiences that should not be missed.

TOP 10 ATTRACTIONS

- **Palazzo Reale** Visit the opulent Palazzo Reale to see how the Savoys lived and played in their days of heady splendour (see pages 63–4)

- **Mole Antonelliana lift** Hop into the glass lift at the Mole Antonelliana for a vertiginous ride and sky-high views over the city (see page 100)

- **Museo Nazionale del Cinema (Cinema Museum)** Film junkies can find their own nirvana at the Cinema Museum, the only one of its kind in the country (see page 105)

- **Palazzo Madama** From a Roman gate to the national senate, take a crash course in Turinese history at Palazzo Madama; be sure not to miss Juvara's stairs (see page 59)

- **Duomo di San Giovanni Battista (The Duomo)** See a replica of the Holy Shroud and pay homage to the real thing at the Duomo di Torino (see pages 76–7)

- **Cafés under the Arcades** Stroll beneath the city's kilometres of arcades, stopping at a pavement café for one of Turin's famous *bicerin* (see pages 86–8)

- **Museo Egizio (Egyptian Museum)** Check out the most extensive collection of Egyptian artefacts outside of Cairo at the world famous Museo Egizio (see page 62)

- **Piedmontese cuisine and wine** Dig into home-cooked Piedmontese cuisine, like traditional *bagna cauda*, or try a glass of renowned Barolo wine (see pages 24–7)

- **Palazzina de Cacciadi Stupinigi (Stupinigi Palace)** Visit the Baroque Stupinigi Palace, former hunting lodge and wedding venue for the royal family, and its sprawling parkland (see page 98)

- **Val d'Aosta** Head out of town to visit Val d'Aosta's Gran Paradiso, the highest mountain group in the nearby Alps (see page 130)

⬤ *The Piazza Reale is at the heart of Turin's sights and attractions*

Suggested itineraries

HALF-DAY: TURIN IN A HURRY

Savour the city on foot, strolling through its arcades (stopping for an espresso or *bicerin* in Caffè San Carlo (see page 68) or one of the other grand old Turinese haunts) and across Piazza Reale, stopping to look inside Palazzo Madama and to stand under San Lorenzo's fabulous dome.

If the Holy Shroud beckons, walk a few steps behind San Lorenzo to the Duomo to see its hiding place – and to glance at the Roman gate and amphitheatre remains, visible from the Duomo's steps. From there, either continue west to wander into the little streets of the Quadrilatero, joining locals for an after-work *aperitivo* and free snacks at a wine bar, or head back through Piazza Reale and down the broad Via Po, stopping for *gelato* at Fiorio before veering left to the Mole Antonelliana for a view of the city and mountains from its glass lift.

1 DAY: TIME TO SEE A LITTLE MORE

The half-day intinerary, above, makes a good route for a full day, but you'll also have the time to tour one or two of the city's most outstanding interiors. Depending on your interests, this could be the Palazzo Reale – for a look at the grandeur that surrounded the Savoy court and to marvel at Juvarra's 'scissor' stairway – or the Museo Egizio, the world's finest Egyptian collection outside of Cairo. Or pay respects to the birthplace of Italian film by visiting the Museo Nazionale del Cinema.

Towards evening, head to the Quadrilatero or stroll on down Via Po to Piazza Vittorio Veneto for the *aperitivo*-with-snacks ritual and dinner. If it's summer, take advantage of your 24 hours by joining the late-night life of the Murazzi.

2–3 DAYS: TIME TO SEE MUCH MORE

With more time, you can explore different neighbourhoods or visit more sights around Piazza Reale, including the Galleria Sabauda and the Museo Nazionale del Risorgimento Italiano, for a tour of the interior of Palazzo Carignano. Break the pace with a stroll in the Giardini Reale behind the palace, and sample several more vintage cafés. Contemporary art mavens can hop a bus to Galleria Civica d'Arte Moderna e Contemporanea (GAM) or to see some of Turin's best modern architecture in the newly revitalised Lingotto district. The Museo dell'Automobile is, appropriately, nearby. Return along the river, through Parco del Valentino and Borgo Medievale. For longer views, cross the Po to the Villa della Regina or take a bus to Sassi for the rack railway ride to Basilica di Superga (use your Torino Card – see page 52). Or take a bus to the suburbs to see showy Stupinigi Palace and its gardens.

For a relaxing break, cruise along the river Po (free with a Torino Card) on the *Valentina* or *Valentino*, from Borgo Medievale or from the Murazzi. Choose a different neighbourhood each evening for your *aperitivo*-followed-by-dinner routine.

And, at least one morning of your stay, make sure you hit the busy market at Porto Palazzo.

LONGER: ENJOYING TURIN TO THE FULL

With more time, you can spend longer exploring neighbourhoods, small museums and churches or take short bus excursions to visit the nearby royal palaces.

For a break from city life, make overnight trips to the mountains west of Turin or to the north, to Gran Paradiso National Park and the Val d'Aosta.

Something for nothing

Home of *aperitivo* wine, Turin has elevated the aperitif-with-snacks to new heights. It may be the day's social highlight for hip Turinese, but for the traveller who brings along a smart outfit, it can mean free dinner. Wine bars outdo each other with spreads of hearty, sophisticated snacks to lure the after-work crowd. Cruise the back streets of the Quadrilatero and order a glass at a wine bar offering

⬤ *Art under the arcades can be free (but he might expect a tip)*

the most interesting (and filling) food. Don't be shy about covering your plate – the locals aren't. For the price of two glasses of wine, you can eat a substantial meal, splitting your grazing between places with the best spreads. Begin early, while the selection is best.

It would be easy to spend a day or two in Turin without ever paying an admission fee. The city's streets, parks and *piazze* are living art museums, with sculpture, exciting architecture, murals, even pavement artists at work under the arcades. From November through to January, the exciting Luci d'Artista illuminates the night with brilliant street art by prominent artists, all created in lights.

On the tourist-sight trail, tour Palazzo Madama free to see Roman remains and one of Juvarra's famous stairways. The Roman amphitheatre and Porta Palatina are free, as are examples of later architecture. Stroll art nouveau neighbourhoods and explore Renzo Piano's re-do of the Lingotto, with a scenic run on its rooftop test track. Return through the riverside Borgo Medievale.

For views, climb the hills across the river to two lofty churches. All the city's churches are free, including Guarini's San Lorenzo, whose dome is among the world's greatest architectural feats. See contemporary art at GAM, free on the first Tuesday of every month; for a week in the spring, all public museums and monuments are also free (check ⓦ www.beniculturali.it for dates).

Festivals mean free concerts, parades and activities, especially the religious/social feasts of the Consolata on June 20 and San Giovanni on 24 June. During the latter everything closes and nighttime fireworks light up the river. Carnevale (usually in February) brings parades, costumed revellers and street performers in the winter, while in the summer you can listen to the music spilling from Murazzi clubs by just sitting on the river bank.

When it rains

With 18 km (11 miles) of arcades, a little rain – or even a lot – doesn't stop the Turinese from the pleasures of window shopping or meeting for a coffee. The sacred *passeggiata* goes on, rain or shine, and the sidewalk tables of many of the city's beloved cafés are protected by the arcades. Along Via Po, they even extend over the crossings of side streets, while those along the sides of Piazza San Carlo have pavements broad enough to serve as 'canvasses' for sidewalk artists, too.

The shelter of these *portici* will take you, largely dry, the entire length of Via Po, between Piazza Reale and Piazza Vittorio Veneto, from Piazza Reale down Via Roma, through Piazza San Carlo and on to Piazza Carlo Felice. Along the way you pass two shopping arcades – including the refurbished 19th-century Galleria Subalpina – as well as the windows of some of the city's most prestigious stores. Via Pietro Micca, Via Cernaia and one side of Corso Vittorio Emanuele II are also covered.

Turin adapts well to bad-weather travel in another way, too. Several of its museums are not only big but they're also varied enough to hold a visitor's attention for several hours. A rainy day gives a traveller the leisure to simply enjoy the moment, to spend a little longer looking at an exhibit or reading the labels. The Museo Nazionale del Cinema could easily occupy half a day with its exhibits, films and interactive displays, and it also has a trendy bar and café.

The 30,000-plus artefacts from the Savoys' hoard in the Museo Egizio take time to see, even if all are not on display at once. Many short-term Turin visitors wisely choose to visit those things more related to the city itself and leave this museum for a rainy day. Likewise, the Museo di Antichità's multi-millennia archaeological dig is also worth burrowing into at leisure.

🔹 *Chic shopping under the arcades: just the place to escape from a shower*

On arrival

TIME DIFFERENCE
Italy follows Central European Time (CET). During Daylight Saving Time (end Mar–end Oct), the clocks go forward one hour.

ARRIVING
By air
The small, modern **Sandro Pertini Airport**, locally known as Caselle (☎ 011 567 6361/2 🅦 www.turin-airport.com), is 16 km (10 miles) north of Turin. Its single terminal handles both arrivals and departures, with tourist information, money exchange, ATM and car hire all right at hand. Taxis (☎ 011 996 3090) wait outside the arrivals hall, taking 30–40 minutes to the city centre, and costing €25–40. In the same time you can take the train to Dora station for about €3 (☎ 011 216 5352 🅦 www.gtt.to.it); trains leave half-hourly from the station attached to the terminal's departures area. Your ticket is good for 70 minutes, covering a connecting bus to your hotel. Buses (☎ 011 300 0611 🅦 www.sadem.it) leave the airport every 30–45 minutes 05.15–23.00, taking about 40 minutes to Porta Nuova railway station, with a stop at Porta Susa. Purchase tickets (€5) at either end of the route or on board.

Milan's **Malpensa Airport** (☎ 02 7485 2200 🅦 www.sea-aeroportimilano.it) is usually the arrival point for travellers from outside Europe, and the SADEM bus is the best way to get to Turin if your flight corresponds to its daily departures at 10.00, 11.30, 14.00, 16.00, 18.30 and 20.30. These leave from Terminal 1, at Exit 4, Stop 18. Tickets cost €18. Alternatively, take the easy shuttle to Milan's Stazione Centrale to catch one of the hourly trains to Turin, at the same combined cost.

By road

The best advice about driving in Turin, at least until the subway construction is completed, is don't. Otherwise, Turin is a very easy city to find your way in, its grid design of streets alternating traffic directions and very few diagonal avenues to confuse the pattern.

Parking is a problem, despite new car parks in the centre, and hotels normally charge extra for parking. It's best to just hire a car when you're ready to leave for the mountains. Routes in and out of the city are wide and well signposted; get driving directions from your hotel if arriving by car. To find a parking space in any of the city's 18 multi-storey car parks, send a text message (SMS) indicating the letter 'P' to 339 994 9990 – the response will show a list of car parks with the number of spaces currently available in each. Or check Ⓦ www.5t.torino.it/5t/it/parcheggi, which gives an up-to-the-minute summary of spaces available in car parks around town.

Turin's bus station is at the corner of Corso Vittorio Emanuele II and Corso Inghilterra, about 600 m (1/2 mile) from Porta Susa (❶ 011 300 0611 Ⓦ www.sadem.it).

By rail

Turin's largest rail station, **Porta Nuova** (❶ 011 669 0246 or toll free in Italy 800 888 088 Ⓦ www.ferroviedellostato.it), at Piazza Carlo Felice, has links to the rest of Europe. It contains the usual big-city rail station amenities – ATM, news-stand, food, and a well-staffed tourist information point. However, Porta Nuova is being eclipsed by smaller **Porta Susa** (❶ 011 562 2535), the terminal for the Eurostar Italia route. Porta Nuova and Porta Susa are connected by Tram 1, and the new subway line. The small **Dora** station (❶ 011 218 8444) serves the airport. Turin's **Lingotto station** (❶ 011 317 3897) is a main

stop for many southbound trains, and is convenient if you're attending one of the city's many trade fairs.

FINDING YOUR FEET

Your first impression of Turin, once past the manufacturing suburbs, is how gracious and beautiful the city is. Much of the centre is lined with arcades, lending a stately air and making walking a pleasure. Your first order of business should be to find a spot in a café under one of the *portici* and begin your acclimatisation to the pace of local life.

It is a fairly safe city, although, as with anywhere else, you should always be aware of your surroundings. Avoid walking – especially alone – late at night in the areas around the stations, Docks Dora or anywhere that looks deserted. And better to save the amorous stroll in the park for daylight. Women will be hassled less in Turin than further south in Italy. Fewer two-wheeled vehicles buzz in and out between cars than in other Italian cities and this makes crossing streets far less stressful.

ORIENTATION

A quick glance at the map on page 57 shows how easy central Turin is to navigate. The majority of major sights are close set, connected by a grid of straight streets and broad *piazze*, so you could stroll past most of them in half a day. Plan your sightseeing to begin in the heart of the Savoys' capital, Piazza Castello. Several major attractions are within sight of this wide plaza, and radiating from it are four streets you will want to explore: Via Roma, Via Po, Via Garibaldi and Via Pietro Micca. If you lose your way, just ask in a shop. The only landmark you're likely to spot as a beacon is the Mole's sharp dome rising to the north of Via Po.

The maps in this book show all the main sights and streets in each area, as well as cafés and restaurants.

GETTING AROUND

A bewildering network of buses and trams connect all parts of Turin, many with a hub at Porta Nuova station. Ask at the airport information kiosk for a transport map, or buy one from any news-stand to be sure of the latest routing, since lines are changing as the subway system begins operating. Bus and tram stops are clearly signposted. Turin's new subway system, partially open, is not much use for sightseeing; although plans are afoot to eventually connect

---

IF YOU GET LOST, TRY …

Excuse me, do you speak English?
Mi scusi, parla inglese?
Mee scoozee, parlah eenglehzeh?

**Excuse me, is this the right way to the old town/
the city centre/the tourist office/the station/
the bus station?**
Mi scusi, questa è la strada giusta per la città vecchia/
il centro/l'ufficio informazioni turistiche/la stazione
ferroviaria/la stazione degli autobus?
*Mee skoozee, kwestah eh lah strahdah justah
pehr la cheetah vehkyah/eel chentroh/loofeecho
eenfohrmahtsyonee tooreesteekah/lah stahtsyoneh
fehrohveeah/lah stahtsyoneh dehlyee owtohboos?*

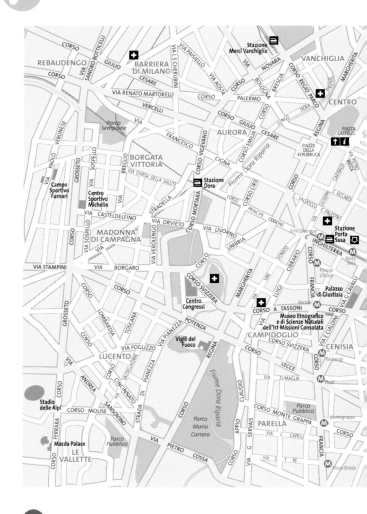

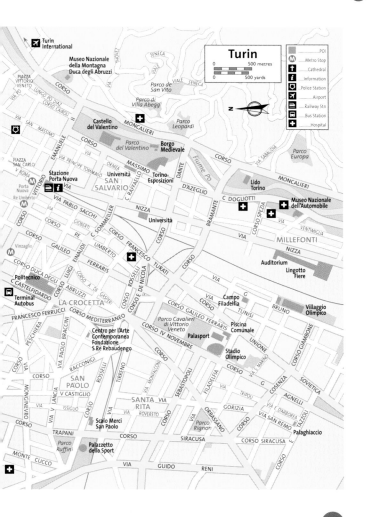

Porta Nuova with the Lingotto complex, don't hold your breath: like everything else in Italy, these things happen slowly!

Bus fares are €0.90, less for strips of ten. You must buy tickets – from any news-stand or tobacconist and in some bars – before climbing aboard. You might want a supply to carry you through Sunday, when many sales points are closed.

Near the front and back of the bus or tram is a validating machine; insert your ticket with the Prima Validation (if applicable) side facing in. Tickets are good for 70 minutes of unlimited transfers. Most lines begin operating at about 05.00, running until 24.00, although not as frequently after 20.00.

Wondering when the next bus will stop? Send a text message (SMS) to 339 994 9990, entering the number (posted prominently) of any of the city's 3,000 bus stops. In a few seconds a reply tells you the next arrival, in real time.

The **Torino + Piemonte Card** combines free bus and tram transport with free admission to 130 major sites in the city and in the Piedmont, including the Mole Antonelliana's glass lift, the Sassi-Superga rack railway and boat rides on the Po. You can start using the card as soon as you arrive, for the airport shuttle into town. Although you may not need to take a lot of buses because plenty of sights are within steps of each other and many, such as churches, are free, major museums and palaces charge €5–8, so if you're planning on seeing several it might be worth investing in a card. You can buy them for €18 (two days), €20 (three days), €30 (five days) or €35 (seven days) at Turismo Torino information points or most hotels.

The Torino TurismoBus (free with the card) makes hourly circuits to 14 major sites, daily 10.00–18.00 from late June to mid-Sept, weekends, special events and holidays in other seasons. Without a Torino Card, the all-day fare is €6. Although easy to use, its hours

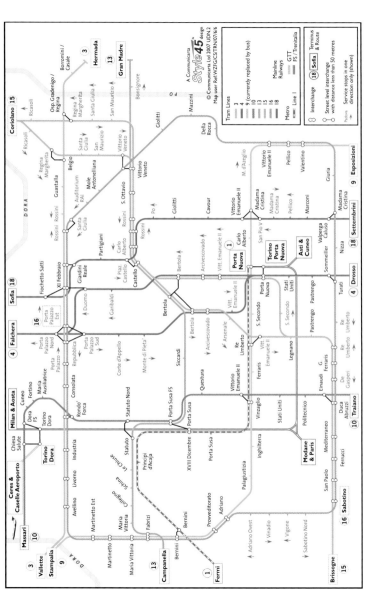

are limited and you may have a long wait for the next circuit. Those staying three days are better off with the Torino Card.

Taxis are plentiful, but regulations do not allow drivers to pick up customers at random points. Go to the nearest taxi rank (look for an orange and black sign), located at train and bus stations, major squares and many hotels. Alternatively, call **Pronto Taxi** (☎ 011 5737) or **Radio Taxi** (☎ 011 5730 or 011 3399). All taxis are metered, with extra charges for luggage, night trips and if you call for a pick-up.

CAR HIRE

While you will not need it in the city, a car is the best way to explore the mountains around Turin. There are ten car-hire agencies at the arrivals hall of Caselle Airport. Link to these directly from the airport website Ⓦ www.turin-airport.com. For quick comparisons, visit Ⓦ www.carrentals.com or Ⓦ www.economycarrentals.com. Check rates before making your flight reservations, as you can often do best with an airline's air-car package, and prices are always cheaper if you've booked ahead of time.

Before leaving the car park, make sure you have all documents and that you know how to operate the vehicle. The main problem is for those from left-hand drive countries, such as the UK and South Africa, but it soon becomes natural as you follow other drivers. Stay alert and ask a passenger to remind you until it becomes customary.

● *The Alps provide a striking background for the Mole Antonelliana*

The Savoy centre

When the ruling Savoy family moved their capital over the Alps from Chambéry, France, to Italy in the 1560s, they wasted no time in remaking the medieval town of Turin into a glittering cosmopolitan city. Piazza Castello was arcaded and by 1584 work had begun on a swanky new 'suburb' laid out grandly along Via Roma. Spacious *piazze* and broad straight avenues became the hallmark of this area, which was further embellished in the baroque era. This grandiose urban sprawl was intended to launch their capital city – and the Savoys themselves – as forces of power and prestige. Thanks to Savoy ambitions, Turin became one of Europe's most regal and beautiful cities, and the Savoys' former royal command centre is at its heart.

SIGHTS & ATTRACTIONS

This Savoy centre is a place for a mellow stroll while admiring the arcaded buildings, broad squares and lush gardens. Many of Turin's sights are clustered around Piazza Castello, several of them in the royal palace itself, so you could easily spend a day visiting them all. But don't overlook the pleasures of joining the Turinese in simply savouring *la dolce vita* in this quarter's cafés, parks and open spaces.

Biblioteca Reale (Royal Library)

It's worth stepping inside just to see the vaulted ceiling. A self-portrait by Leonardo da Vinci is kept here, and is occasionally on exhibit. ❸ Piazza Castello ❶ 011 543 855 ❷ 08.15–18.45 Mon & Wed, 08.15–13.45 Tues, Thur–Sat, closed Sun ❷ Bus/Tram: 4, 11, 12, 13, 15, 18, 27, 51, 55, 56, 57, 63, 72

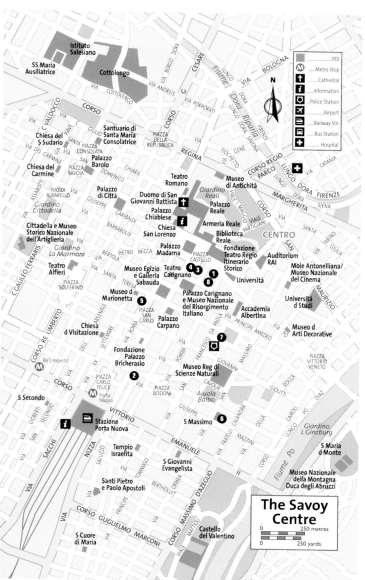

CHIESA DI SAN LORENZO (CHURCH OF SAN LORENZO)

Guarino Guarini designed this church, whose austere exterior (like that of the palace it adjoins) gives no clue to the riot of baroque inside, nor to its interior shape. Although often described as octagonal, the round-domed centre is actually surrounded by eight curved bays. Considered one of the world's great churches architecturally, and described by one Guarini scholar as 'a great work of hallucinatory engineering', San Lorenzo's fame rests in its dome and lantern, which is carried aloft on a delicate cage of intersecting ribs. ➌ Piazza Castello ☎ 011 4361 527 ◷ 07.30–12.00, 16.00–19.30 Mon–Sat, 09.00–13.00, 16.00–19.30, 20.30–22.00 Sun ☒ Bus/Tram: 4, 11, 12, 13, 15, 18, 27, 51, 55, 56, 57, 63, 72

Giardini Reali (Royal Gardens)

Designed at the end of the 17th century by the same landscape artist who created those at Versailles (the Savoys were influenced in their choices by the French court), the upper gardens contain a fountain full of tritons and sea nymphs. The intimate and charming lower gardens are accessible from an entrance off Corso San Maurizio or from Viale 1 Maggio. ➋ Entrance on Viale Luzio ◷ 09.00–one hr before sunset ☒ Bus/Tram: 3, 4, 11, 12, 13, 15, 16, 18, 27, 51, 55, 56, 57, 63, 72

Palazzo Carignano

Designed by baroque master architect Guarino Guarini, this massive palace is made of bricks fired in a kiln right at the construction site, so Guarini would have just the right shapes for the curving facade.

Look for the designs inspired by tales of American Indians recounted to the Savoy court by a contemporary adventurer. The first king of United Italy, Victor Emanuele II, was born here, and the palace contains the chamber of deputies where the first Italian Parliament met. (See Risorgimento Museum, pages 62–3.) ❷ Via Accademia delle Scienze 5 (off Via Lagrange) ❶ 011 562 1147 ❸ 09.00–19.00 Tues–Sat, 09.00–13.00 Sun ❹ Bus/Tram: 4, 11, 12, 13, 15, 18, 27, 51, 55, 56, 57, 63, 72

Palazzo di Città

Stop by Turin's baroque city hall to check out Corrado Levi and the Cliostradt Group's contemporary artwork, *Baci Urbani (Urban Kisses) – Piercing*. A giant steel loop pierces the corner of an 18th-century building, complete with dripping blue blood. ❸ Via Palazzo di Città 19 ❹ Bus/Tram: 4, 11, 12, 27, 51, 57

Palazzo Madama

Think of this building – which you can hardly miss in the centre of the piazza – as one-stop shopping for the history of Turinese architecture. Beginning with the towers of the Roman Porta Pretoria, it includes a 15th-century castle of Ludovico D'Acaja (on the Po River side), a baroque western façade and monumental staircase, all capped off by a tower of unmistakable Fascist design added in the 1930s. However incongruous, it is a striking building, and you can just walk in whenever the doors are open to see the inside and learn more about its history from a free video. Highlights are Roman remains and Filippo Juvarra's grand staircase. ❸ Piazza Castello ❶ 011 443 3501 ❿ www.palazzomadamatorino.it ❸ 09.00–19.00 Tues–Fri & Sun, 09.00–20.00 Sat ❹ Bus/Tram: 4, 11, 12, 13, 15, 18, 27, 51, 55, 56, 57, 63, 72. Admission charge for some areas

Piazza Castello

When Duke Emanuele Filiberto moved his capital to the small mercantile crossroads of Turin in the late 1500s, he immediately began rearranging it into a modern city worthy of the Savoy presence. Although the general shape and size of the square was determined by Emanuele's early architects, the piazza continued to take form over the next two centuries, culminating in the baroque additions of Filippo Juvarra – the west facade of Palazzo Madama and the

⬤ *Duke Emanuele Filiberto rides across Piazza San Carlo*

state archives. Now traffic-free, the open space is studded with benches from which to admire the buildings. Bus/Tram: 4, 11, 12, 13, 15, 18, 27, 51, 55, 56, 57, 63, 72

Piazza San Carlo

Lined up perfectly with Piazza Castello, this is the second of the grand squares of the old Savoy centre. Three sides are framed in arcades, and the fourth maintains this symmetry with a matched pair of church façades, San Carlo Borromeo and Santa Cristina. In the centre of the piazza stands a statue of Duke Emanuele Filiberto on horseback, after his 1557 victory at San Quentino. Under the arcades are two of Turin's most famous and elegant cafés (see page 68). Bus/Tram: 1, 4, 9, 11, 12, 15, 18, 51, 55, 56, 67, 68

Via Po

Wide enough for three carriages to ride abreast, Via Po was a marvel of its day. Arcades protect pedestrians on either side, extending over crossings of side streets. Above them rises a uniform line of three-storey buildings, all the result of a strict city planning requirement of Carlo Emanuele's court architect. Peek into the courtyard of the university as you pass number 15. Bus/Tram: 1, 4, 9, 11, 12, 13, 15, 18, 51, 55, 56, 61, 67, 68

CULTURE

Inside some of the buildings mentioned above, and others in the Savoy centre, are museums that house Turin's artistic and historic treasures. Some are for enthusiasts of the subject – ancient Egypt, antique weaponry, the *Risorgimento* – and others are palaces that illuminate court life in the glory days of the Savoys.

Armeria Reale (Royal Armoury)

Displayed in a section of the Palazzo Reale is one of the finest collections of weaponry and armour in Europe. Look out for the equine armour worn by Emanuele Filiberto's horse in the statue on Piazza San Carlo. ② Piazza Castello 191 ① 011 543 889 ⑩ www.ambienteto.arti.beniculturali.it ⑤ 09.00–14.00 Tues–Fri, 13.00–19.00 Sat & Sun, closed Mon ⑩ Bus/Tram: 4, 11, 12, 13, 15, 18, 27, 51, 55, 56, 57, 63, 72

Museo Egizio (Egyptian Museum)

Only the museum in Cairo has a more complete collection of artefacts from Egyptian civilisation before the 6th century. Exhibits, which range from state-of-the-art interpretations to bizarrely random cabinets of curiosities, include a highly regarded statue of Ramses II and a collection of mummies and funerary finds. ② Via Accademia delle Scienze 6 ① 011 5617 776 ⑩ www.museoegizio.org ⑤ 08.30–19.30 Tues–Sun, closed Mon, mid-Sept–mid-June; 09.30–20.30 Tues–Sun, closed Mon, mid-June–mid-Sept ⑩ Bus/Tram: 4, 11, 12, 13, 15, 18, 27, 51, 55, 56, 57, 63, 72

Museo Nazionale del Risorgimento Italiano (National Museum of Italian Unification)

Set inside Palazzo Carignano, designed by Guarino Guarini, the museum is worth entering for the palace itself, let alone the story of Italy's birth as a modern nation. A film in English gives a good background on the times, in which the ever-present Savoys played an important role. You can also see the room where the first Italian Parliament met, in the brief period during which Turin was the capital of the country. The museum was due to open at the end of 2007/beginning of 2008, with the following expected opening times. ② Via Accademia delle

> ### GALLERIA SABAUDA
> Paintings from the royal family's collections have been
> supplemented with later gifts, resulting in a fine display,
> especially strong on the Flemish and Dutch masters,
> including Van Eyck, Rembrandt, Van Dyck and Jan Brueghel.
> ② Via Accademia delle Scienze 6 ① 011 547 440
> ⓦ www.museitorino.it ⓛ 08.30–14.00 Tues, 14.00–19.30 Wed,
> 10.00–19.30 Thur, 08.30–14.00 Fri–Sun, closed Mon
> ⓝ Bus/Tram: 13, 15, 18, 55, 56, 63, 72

Scienze 5 (off Via Lagrange) ① 011 562 1147 ⓦ www.regione.piemonte.it
ⓛ 09.00–19.00 Tues-Sun, closed Mon ⓝ Bus/Tram: 4, 11, 12, 13, 15, 18,
27, 51, 55, 56, 57, 63, 72

Palazzo Bricherasio
Totally restored over five years, the 17th-century home of
Countess Sofia di Bricherasio presents a luxurious peek at times
past. ② Via Lagrange 20 ① 011 571 1811 ⓦ www.palazzobricherasio.it
ⓛ 14.30–19.30 Mon; 09.30–19.30 Tues, Wed, Fri & Sun, 09.30–22.30
Thur & Sat ⓝ Bus/Tram: 4, 11, 12, 13, 15, 18, 27, 51, 55, 56, 57, 63, 72.
Admission charge

Palazzo Reale (Royal Palace)
Once the nerve centre of the Savoys' command zone, the exterior of
the Palazzo Reale makes up for its simplicity in sheer size. By contrast,
the interior is decked out in an almost overwhelming display of
baroque courtly splendour, befitting the lordly Savoys. The palace's
piano nobile (first floor) is open only for guided tours in Italian, but

signs in English describe the contents of the rooms – if you can read as fast as the guides can talk. The Salone degli Svizzeri, the hang-out of the palace's Swiss Guards, is decorated with frescoes (the work of Giovanni Francesco and Antonio Fea) portraying the Savoy family genealogy. The ballroom is encrusted with decoration, its ceiling covered in a fresco of Olympus. This opulence is echoed in the smaller (but hardly intimate) throne room, where band after band of ornate cornice moulding frames the ceiling. The crowning artistic achievement of the palace is the Scala delle Forbici, Juvarra's 'scissor' stairway. ⓐ Piazzetta Reale ❶ 011 4361 455 ⓦ www.ambienteto.arti.beniculturali.it ⓛ 08.30–19.30 Tues–Sun, closed Mon; visits by guided tour only, last tour begins 18.15 ⓝ Bus/Tram: 4, 11, 12, 13, 15, 18, 27, 51, 55, 56, 57, 63, 72

Teatro Regio

Backstage tours of the opera house – which last 90 minutes – include costume rooms, set storage, rehearsal rooms, the dome and the stage, where rehearsals are often in progress. A rare opportunity to see areas that are normally closed to the public. ⓐ Piazza Castello 215 ❶ 011 881 5209 ⓦ www.teatroregio.torino.it ⓛ Guided tours 15.00 Sat, Sept–July by advance reservation only ⓝ Bus/Tram: 4, 11, 12, 13, 15, 18, 27, 51, 55, 56, 57, 63, 72

RETAIL THERAPY

They're all here, under the arcades of Via Roma: Hermès, Gucci, Prada, Armani, Ferragamo. Unless you're dressed the part and look like you're going to buy something, you may find sales clerks in some of these stores looking down their aquiline noses at you. If you're on a budget, but still intent on downtown shopping, browse in nearby chains like

Zara and H&M. Most shops in this area are closed Monday morning; some all day Sunday.

Juventus Store An essential stop for football fanatics. ❷ Via Garibaldi 4/E
🕐 011 433 8709 🐸 www.juventustore.com 🕐 15.30–19.30 Mon,
10.00–19.30 Tues–Sat, closed Sun ❷ Bus/Tram: 4, 11, 12, 27, 51, 57

Mood Relax with a book and a fine cup of Italian coffee at this trendy
little bookstore and café. ❷ Via Cesare Battisti 3/E 🕐 011 566 0809
🐸 www.moodlibri.it 🕐 10.00–21.00 Mon–Sat, closed Sun ❷ Bus/Tram:
4, 11, 12, 13, 15, 18, 27, 51, 55, 56, 57, 63, 72

Oasi dei Prodotti Tipici della Campagna Piemontese Hit this Sunday
market to pick up a wide range of typical Piedmontese products to
take back home. ❷ Piazza Palazzo di Città 🕐 First Sun of every month
(except Jan, July, Aug) ❷ Bus/Tram: 4, 11, 12, 27, 51, 57 or ❷ Piazza Madama
Cristina 🕐 third Sun of every month (except July, Aug & Dec)
❷ Bus/Tram: 1. 9, 18, 34, 35, 52, 66, 67

RAO Strictly for the privileged set, RAO has featured top-quality
women's clothing since 1956. The male equivalent is nearby, at
Via Andrea Doria 8 ❷ Via Lagrange 6 (at Via Cavour) 🕐 011 562 1298
🕐 15.00–19.30 Mon, 10.00–19.30 Tues–Sat, closed Sun ❷ Bus/Tram:
1, 18, 61, 68

Stratta Seducing local taste buds since 1836, historic Stratta is famous
for its Turineis, chocolates with a chestnut and rum cream filling, among
many other confections. ❷ Piazza San Carlo 191 🕐 011 547 920
🐸 www.stratta1836.it 🕐 15.00–19.30 Mon, 09.30–13.00, 15.00–19.30
Tues–Sat, closed Sun ❷ Bus/Tram: 4, 11, 12, 15, 27, 57, 58, 63

TAKING A BREAK

Under the arcades of *piazze* San Carlo and Castello are the city's ritziest and most venerable cafés, and it would be criminal to visit Turin without sampling at least one of them. As much a part of Turin as FIAT and the Shroud – and to many, even more holy – the cafés are the weft of its gastronomic, architectural, historical and social fabric. Whatever table you choose, you can be certain that the elbows of an important musician, statesman, writer, artist or bon vivant rested there before yours – or will rest there next week.

Fiorio £ ❶ Although some of the decor's splendour may have faded, its *gelato* is as creamy as when the Savoys smacked their royal lips over it. Reputed to be the best cream *gelati* in Italy, a claim we can't dispute. Order their speciality – a three-scoop combo of chocolate, pistachio and vanilla. ➌ Via Po 8 ☎ 011 817 3225 ⓦ www.fioriocaffegelateria.com ◷ Tues–Sun, closed Mon Ⓝ Bus/Tram: 13, 15, 55, 56

Gertosio/La Baita del Formaggio £ ❷ This bakery/chocolate shop and next-door deli make such a good team that it can't be by accident. For a picnic lunch, buy bread at one and filling at the other. Gertosio ➌ Via Lagrange 34 ☎ 011 562 1942 ⓦ www.pasticceriagertosio.it ◷ 08.00–13.00, 15.30–19.30 Tues–Sat, closed Sun; La Baita del Formaggio ➌ Via Lagrange 36 ☎ 011 562 3224 ◷ 09.00–13.00, 16.00–19.30 Tues–Sat, closed Mon Ⓝ Bus/Tram: 1, 18, 61, 68

▶ Stile Liberty – *art nouveau style – can even be found in shops*

Arcadia ££ ❸ In the 19th-century covered shopping gallery off Piazza Castello, Arcadia is a funky little Italian/Japanese eatery, handy for a quick lunch stop while touring the Savoy sights. Choose from pasta, all of which is made fresh in-house, or one of the fabulous mixed sushi menus. ⓐ Galleria Subalpina ❶ 011 561 3898 Ⓦ www.ristorantearcadia.com ❶ 12.30–14.30, 20.00–22.30 Mon–Sat, closed Sun Ⓝ Bus/Tram: 4, 11, 12, 13, 15, 18, 27, 51, 55, 56, 57, 63, 72

Caffè Baratti & Milano ££ ❹ Best known for its aperitifs and sandwiches, this Turin institution also serves full lunches. It was a favourite of the Savoy royals. ⓐ Piazza Castello 27 (at the entrance to the Gallerie Subalpina) ❶ 011 440 7138 ❶ Lunch 12.30–14.30, Café service 08.00–01.00 Tues–Sun, closed Mon Ⓝ Bus/Tram: 4, 11, 12, 13, 15, 18, 27, 51, 55, 56, 57, 63, 72

Caffè San Carlo ££ ❺ With the distinction of being the first café in Italy (maybe in Europe) to be lit by gas, this elegant café was the haunt of *Risorgimento* patriots, who nibbled the delectable San Carlo almond cake as they plotted. You can, too, while admiring one of the finest plaster work and gilt interiors in the city. ⓐ Piazza San Carlo 156 ❶ 011 532 586 Ⓦ www.caffesancarlo.it ❶ Meals 12.00–15.00, 19.00–23.00, Café service 08.00–4.00 Ⓝ Bus/Tram: 1, 4, 9, 11, 12, 15, 18, 51, 55, 56, 67, 68, 72

AFTER DARK

Strolling through the arcades is the best way to begin an evening, perhaps with a stop as the Turinese do, for an *aperitivo* (and pre-dinner snacks!) in one of the cafés. Buildings in this area are lavishly illuminated at night, especially the Palazzo Madama and others in Piazza Castello. Some of the elegant cafés, including the Caffè San Carlo (see page 68), serve dinner, providing another chance to enjoy their sumptuous interiors.

RESTAURANTS

L'Agrifoglio ££ ❻ Try this tiny, local favourite for traditional ambience and modern interpretations of Piedmont classics, including *agnolotti* (local ravioli) and rabbit marinated in onions and cloves. ❷ Via Provano Andrea 7 (near Corso Vittorio Emanuele II end of street) ❶ 011 813 6837 ❸ 19.00–23.00 Tues–Sat, closed Sun & Mon ❷ Bus/Tram: 9, 18, 34, 35, 52, 61, 67, 68

La Badessa ££ ❼ Dine amid antiques inside the noble Palazzo Coardi di Carpeneto, or outside overlooking the piazza, on traditional Piedmontese recipes created by the Mother Superior and great chef, Maria Caterina Operti, over a century ago. The religious ate well, and so will you, on main courses such as swordfish with saffron rice cakes or grilled veal stuffed with fontina cheese and herbs. ❷ Piazza Carlo Emanuele II 17 ❶ 011 835 940 ❿ www.labadessa.net ❸ 19.30–23.30 Mon, 12.00–14.30, 19.30–23.30 Tues–Sun ❷ Bus/Tram: 13, 15, 55, 56

Sfashion Café ££ ❽ This place does some of the best pizza in Turin. With outdoor seating, excellent daily specials and home-made pastas, it's popular, so get there early if you want to snag a table on the piazza. ❷ Via Cesare Battisti 13, Piazza Carlo Alberto ❶ 011 516 0085 ❿ www.sfashioncafe.it ❸ Bar 08.00–01.00, Restaurant 12.30–14.30, 19.30–23.30, Pizza served 12.30–15.00, 19.30–24.00 Mon–Fri, 12.30–24.00 Sat & Sun ❷ Bus/Tram: 13, 15, 55, 56

CINEMAS & THEATRES

Cinema Romano Three small cinemas in one, showing current releases, mostly blockbusters. ❸ Galleria Subalpina, Piazza Castello 9 ❶ 011 562 0145 ⓦ www.mymovies.it ⓝ Bus/Tram: 4, 11, 12, 13, 15, 18, 27, 51, 55, 56, 57, 63, 72

Teatro Gobetti Prose theatre productions, occasionally in English, by touring Italian and foreign companies. ❷ Via Rossini 8 ❶ 011 8159 132; Box office ❸ Via Roma 49 ❶ 011 5176 246/011 5637 079 (toll-free from Italy 800 235 333) ⓦ www.teatrostabiletorino.it ⓝ Bus/Tram: 13, 15, 18, 55, 56,68

Teatro Regio The two theatres in Piazza Castello, Teatro Regio and Piccolo Regio, present a wide range of musical events, including opera,

◗ *Hitting the floor at one of Turin's many lively clubs*

ballet, symphony and vocal concerts. Giacomo Puccini's *La Bohème* premièred in the Piccolo Regio. Opening nights need to be booked early, but tickets are usually available the same day for other performances. ⓐ Piazza Castello 215 ⓣ 011 881 5241 ⓦ www.teatroregio.torino.it ⓝ Bus/Tram: 4, 11, 12, 13, 15, 18, 27, 51, 55, 56, 57, 63, 72

Torino Spettacoli Check with Torino Spettacoli for the latest in avant-garde theatre, primarily at Teatro Alfieri (see page 92), Teatro Erba and Teatro Gioiello. The website often lists special offers, such as four tickets for one euro each. Shows primarily in Italian. ⓐ Offices: Corso Moncalieri 241 ⓣ 011 661 8404 ⓦ www.torinospettacoli.com

BARS, CLUBS & DISCOS
Pastis Popular with people of all ages, Pastis' 1950s French-inspired interior blends perfectly with the 1970s 'regular bar' feel of the place. Free snacks are whipped up using the best quality, freshest ingredients, and a small room features rotating exhibitions of local artists. ⓐ Piazza Emanuele Filiberto 9 ⓣ 011 521 1085 ⓛ 09.00–02.00 ⓝ Bus/Tram: 3, 16 ⓘ closest stop is at the west end of Piazza della Repubblica

Scapadacà A combination of an *aperitivo* spot, cocktail bar and club, this new arrival on Turin's late-night scene is already a favourite with the university crowd. Music is cutting-edge – most DJs are local – and prices are reasonable. ⓐ Corso San Maurizio 48/B ⓣ 011 812 6515 ⓛ 19.00–03.00 Mon–Fri, 19.00–04.00 Sat & Sun ⓝ Bus/Tram: 15, 16, 30, 55

The Quadrilatero & Cittadella

While the Savoys' building boom reshaped everything east of the Duomo with new broad avenues and *piazze*, the area to the west was allowed to evolve pretty much on its own. As a result, no one style dominates to the west of Via Roma. The city's oldest churches – and oldest structures of any kind – are in the Quadrilatero, where you will find Roman buildings and the city's only medieval buildings. As you roam south into Cittadella, you'll discover remnants of the 1500s citadel, plus every building style since, from baroque to art nouveau and contemporary, in an interesting, eclectic jumble. This area is definitely up-and-coming, and a visit to Turin wouldn't be complete without an evening joining the throngs teeming among its bars and restaurants.

SIGHTS & ATTRACTIONS

The Duomo, which seems to turn its back on the Savoy command centre even though it was very much a part of it, is a good place to begin exploring the area known as the Quadrilatero Romano. It extends north to Piazza della Repubblica, beyond which is the newly revitalised Docks Dora area. Via Garibaldi leads west, and to the south is the Cittadella, former site of the 16th-century walled fortress. Here, and further south, are some of Turin's most striking examples of art nouveau.

Art nouveau buildings

To find *Stile Liberty* (art nouveau, see box on page 82) buildings, wander Corso Francia from Piazza Statuto, looking up to spot curving windows, floral (and sometimes florid) decoration, sweeping reverse

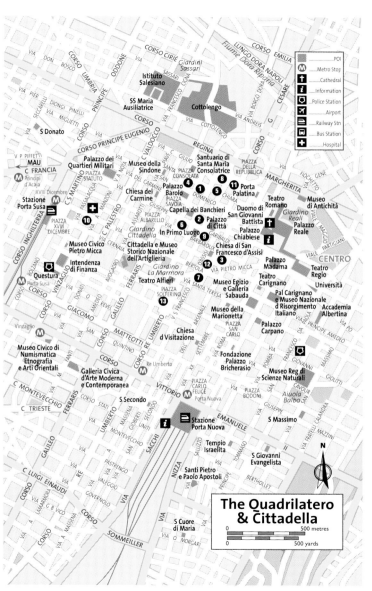

curves and asymmetrical forms typical of the style. Some better-known examples are at the corners of Via Principe d'Acaja and Via Bagetti, and at no. 23 Corso Francia. Other streets in the neighbourhood have outstanding examples, too: look for the wrought-iron work on Via Piffetti 3–5; if you're hooked after this sampler, seek out Casa Florio on via San Francesco d'Assisi 17, Casa Avezzano on Via Giovanni Battista Vico 2 (at Via Andrea Massena), Casa Sigismondi at Via Madama Cristina 5, and two on Corso Ferraris at nos 22 and 78. Or, without wandering from the beaten path at all, you can sample the style at Palazzo Bellia, Via Pietro Micca nos 4–8, between Piazza Solferino and Piazza Castello.

Cappella della Pia Congregazione dei Banchieri e dei Mercanti (Chapel of the Pious Congregation of Bankers & Merchants)

One of Turin's best-kept secrets, this baroque gem is hidden behind a cloister, Antichi Chiostri. Built in 1692 for the Pious Congregation of Merchants & Bankers and dedicated to the three wise men, the chapel's highlight is a vaulted ceiling painted in frescoes by Legnanino. ⓐ Via Garibaldi 25 ⓣ 011 562 7226 ⓛ 15.00–18.00 Sat, 10.00–12.00 Sun, closed Mon–Fri, Sept–June; closed July & Aug, Mass 11.00 Sun ⓝ Bus/Tram: 4, 11, 12, 27, 50, 57

Chiesa di Corpus Domini (Church of the Lord's Body)

The altarpiece depicts the story of a French soldier who stole a chalice containing a consecrated host from a church in Val di Susa in 1453, but when he tried to sell it in Turin, the chalice jumped from his pack and suspended itself in the air just out of reach. The spot where this happened was commemorated by this church 150 years later, by which

● *The sumptuous home of the Holy Shroud*

time the Duomo had already claimed the chalice. It remains there today, and is used every year on Maundy Thursday. The church's rich and colourful marble interior was completed in the mid-1700s.
ⓐ Piazza Corpus Domini (Via San Tommaso at Via Municipio)
ⓘ 011 436 6025 ⓒ 07.30–11.30, 15.00–18.00, closed afternoons in Aug, Mass 07.30 Mon–Sat, 17.30 Thur, 10.00 Sun ⓝ Bus/Tram: 4, 11, 12, 27, 50, 57

Chiesa di San Francesco d'Assisi (Church of St Francis of Assisi)
The original convent church was built in the 1300s, and was home to the Holy Shroud during 16th-century repairs to the Duomo. In this church, St John Bosco (founder of the Salesian Order, which rescues and educates abandoned children) celebrated his first mass after his ordination. It was also here that he met the child who inspired his establishment of the Salesian Order. ⓐ Via San Francesco d'Assisi 11
ⓘ 011 562 8474 ⓒ 07.00–13.00, 15.30–19.30 Mon–Sat, 09.00–12.00, 16.30–20.00 Sun, Mass 18.45 Mon–Sat, 19.15 Sun ⓝ Bus/Tram: 4, 11, 12, 27, 51 57

Duomo di San Giovanni Battista (Cathedral)
Although the cathedral is best known as the location of the Holy Shroud (La Sacra Sindone), this religious relic actually has its own home, in the Cappella della Sacra Sindone, a separate chapel between the church and the Savoy palace. Although it is rarely on view (the next showing is scheduled for 2025), a replica is displayed near the entrance to the church.

Above the entrance is a copy of da Vinci's *The Last Supper* commissioned by Savoy Duke Carlo Felice and presented to the Duomo by Carlo Alberto. In the second altar on the right is a noteworthy series of panels from a 16th-century painted altarpiece. The building itself is the only major Renaissance work remaining in Turin, dating from the 1490s. The façade is decorated by carved marble panels that surround the doors. ⓐ Piazza San Giovanni ⓣ 011 436 1540 ⓛ 07.00–12.30, 15.00–19.00 Mon–Sat, 08.00–12.00, 15.00–19.00 Sun, Mass 07.00, 18.00 Mon–Sat, 09.00, 10.30, 18.00 Sun ⓜ Bus/Tram: 4, 11, 12, 27, 51, 57

Palazzo dei Quartieri Militari

Built between 1716 and 1728, the symmetrical Military Quarters were constructed at the western entrance to the city, Porta Susina. The Museum of the Resistance, Deportation, War, Rights & Freedom, documenting the role of Turin and its citizens during World War II, is housed in one wing of the building. The multimedia library is open to the public, and stocks extensive information about the history of the city. ⓐ Corso Valdocco 4 ⓣ 011 436 1433 ⓦ www.museodiffusotorino.it ⓛ Museum 10.00–18.00 Tues & Wed, Fri–Sun, 14.00–22.00 Thur, closed Mon ⓜ Bus/Tram: 13, 72

Palazzo Falletti di Barolo

Step in to see the central staircase and foyer of this patrician home of a Marchesa. You'll need an appointment to see the rooms of the *piano nobile*, which give a good idea as to the lifestyle of 17th-century Turinese aristrocracy. ⓐ Via delle Orfane 7 ⓣ 011 436 0311 ⓦ www.palazzobarolo.it ⓛ 10.00–12.00, 15.00–17.00 Mon & Wed, 10.00–12.00 Fri, 15.30–18.30 Sun, closed Tues, Thur & Sat, Sept–July; 10.00–12.00 Mon, Wed & Fri, closed Tues, Thur, Sat & Sun, Aug ⓜ Bus/Tram: 3, 16, 52, 60. Admission charge

Piazza Consolata

A small square, but a busy one, with Turin's best-loved church and a venerable café where the city's signature drink – the *bicerin* (see page 88) – was invented. In good weather, café tables, outdoor music and strolling locals share the limited space. In the small streets off the piazza are wine bars and independent shops.

🚌 Bus/Tram: 3, 16, 52, 60

⬤ *The city's Roman origins are still visible*

Piazza Solferino

Nineteenth-century buildings surround the piazza, including Palazzo Ceriena and Teatro Alfiera. In its centre, next to a 1930 fountain of the four seasons, is the ultra-modern – and highly controversial – Atrium Torino, built in 2004 to herald the city's transformation for the 2006 Winter Olympics. The future of the wood, glass and steel structure after the Olympics seemed uncertain, but locals have accepted it, and it now serves serves quite nicely as a tourist information point and display space. ❷ Via Pietra Micca connects this long, busy piazza to Piazza Castello ❷ Bus/Tram: 4, 11, 12, 13, 15, 27, 29, 51, 57, 65, 72

In Primo Luogo

Pop into the indoor shopping area off Via Garibaldi and allow yourself be drawn into Piedmontese artist Michelangelo Pistoletto's installation – a copy of the Etruscan statue of Aulus Metellus (L'Arringatore, or Orator, the original of which is in Florence's Archaeological Museum), positioned in front of a huge mirror. ❷ Centro Commerciale Garibaldi, entrance on Via Garibaldi 18 ❷ Bus/Tram: 4, 11, 12, 27, 51, 57

Porta Palatina

Near the remains of Roman walls stands the imposing gate, the only remaining of the four entrances to the Roman city of Augusta Taurinorum. Built in the 1st century AD, it is one of the best preserved Roman gates in the world. Constructed of brick, it has two polygonal towers connected by a three-storey wall. During the two centuries since it was built, the gate has been used as a noble residence and a prison for women. Legend holds that the Emperor Charlemagne camped here in 773. The statues of Caesar and Augustus are not originals. ❷ Via XX Settembre ❷ Bus/Tram: 4, 11, 12, 27, 51, 57

Santuario di Santa Maria Consolatrice (La Consolata)

Virtually nothing remains in Turin of the period under the Franks, from 773 to 940, with the exception of the campanile of the Benedictine church of Sant'Andrea, which was preserved by Guarini when he rebuilt it in 1678 as a sanctuary dedicated to Mary. In 1729 Filippo Juvarra added the oval presbytery; check out the room to its left to see the collection of paintings and artworks in which faithful church members have depicted their brushes with death. ❸ Piazza della Consolata ❶ 011 436 3235 ❹ 06.30–19.30, Mass every half hour 06.30–12.00 Mon–Sat, every hour 06.00–12.00, 18.15–19.30 Sun ❷ Bus/Tram: 3, 16, 52, 60

Teatro Romano (Roman Amphitheatre)

The Roman city was variously incorporated, removed, covered or left in place, so the area north of Via Garibaldi – the Romans' *decimus maximus* – still has a smattering of remains from that era. Among them is part of the amphitheatre, the rest of which was covered over by the royal palace complex. The open-air site next to the Duomo is fenced, so you can't wander about its ancient stones, but it is fully visible. ❸ Via XX Settembre 89, Piazza San Giovanni ❷ Bus/Tram: 4, 11, 12, 27, 51, 57

Via Garibaldi

Leading west from Palazzo Madama, the street was designed in 1775, following the route of the Roman *decimus maximus*. Today it is a pedestrianised kilometre of shops. To meet three-quarters of Turin's population, go there on a Saturday afternoon. ❷ Bus/Tram: 4, 11, 12, 27, 51 57

CULTURE

The museums of this district are more widely scattered than those around the Palazzo Reale, but the streets between them are so filled with funky shops, wine bars and eye-catching architecture that you won't mind the distances.

Galleria Civica d'Arte Moderna e Contemporanea (GAM)

Interesting exhibits compare works of local avant-garde luminaries with their more famous contemporaries. The time period stretches from the 18th to the 21st century and the collections are primarily Italian but also include works by Paul Klee, Max Ernst and other noteworthies. ⓐ Via Magenta 31 ⓣ 011 506 9052 ⓦ www.gamtorino.it ⓛ 10.00–18.00 Tues–Sun, closed Mon ⓝ Bus/Tram: 1, 64

MAU – Museo di Arte Urbana (Museum of Urban Art)

Murals and installations by local artists. All artworks are dotted around the former workers' quarter at the west end of the Quadrilatero. Keep your eyes peeled as you wander through the streets between Corso Tassoni, Via Amadeo Peyron and Corso Francia, or check the website if you're looking for a specific artwork. ⓐ Borgo Vecchio Campodiglio (offices at Via Musinè 19) ⓣ 011 745 580 ⓦ www.arte2000.net/mau ⓝ Bus/Tram: 3, 13, 16

Museo Civico Pietro Micca

The tale of Pietro Micca blowing up the tunnel – and himself in the process – to prevent French attackers from entering via the subterranean passageways under the Citadel is a familiar one to every Piedmont schoolchild. This and the story of the siege of 1706 are recounted here, but the best part is that you can tour the actual tunnels. The

THE NEW LOOK

The art nouveau style rocked European art and architecture at the turn of the 20th century, with bold new shapes and designs that shocked the stuffy traditionalists of the art establishment. The new look delighted the rising moneyed class of new industrialists, who were looking for ways to carve their own niche in society – and in Turin. With its new car plants springing up, the city had plenty of these entrepreneurs, who were keen to mark their own turf in central Turin, where the old Savoy cronies still held sway. Nothing could have suited this brash crowd of movers and doers better than a fresh and flamboyant look for their houses.

The General Exposition held in Turin in 1902 was just the inspiration they needed, as the foremost architects and artists strutted their newest stuff: flowing lines, deep curves, decorated tiles, floral and nature themes all translated well onto architectural materials. So art nouveau – called *Stile Liberty* in Italy – became the new look for the previously undeveloped areas close to the old centre – Corso Francia (beyond Porta Susa rail station) via Cibrario (the westward continuance of Via Garibaldi), the Crocetta (south of Corso Vittorio Emanuele) and the hillside just across the Po.

model of Turin in the 1700s, when the walls still enclosed this whole part of the city, is interesting, too. ❷ Via Guicciardini 7 ❶ 011 546 317 ❶ www.comune.torino.it/musei ❶ 09.00–19.00 Tues–Sun, closed Mon. Tunnel tours half-hourly morning, hourly afternoon ❶ Bus/Tram: 1, 10, 55, 65. Admission charge

Museo della Marionetta Piemontese

Thousands of strung marionettes and hand puppets along with stages, costumes and other puppetiana have been collected by the Lupi family of puppeteers. Since the 1700s the family has not only presented marionette theatre, but has worked to keep the traditions alive. The museum includes a theatre with regular performances.
ⓐ Via Santa Teresa 5 ⓣ 011 530 238 ⓛ 09.00–13.00, 14.00–17.00 Mon–Fri, closed Sat & Sun, Sept–July; closed Aug ⓝ Bus/Tram: 1, 4, 9, 11, 12, 15, 18, 51, 55, 56, 61, 67, 68. Admission charge

Museo della Sindone (Museum of the Holy Shroud)

The crypt of the San Sudario di Torino church is the site of a museum that examines the history, science, religion and art of one of Christendom's most celebrated and controversial relics. Since it's run by a religious confraternity – the Brotherhood of the Holy Shroud – it's not a place you're likely to find cutting-edge theories debunking the Shroud's authenticity, but the notion of constantly changing 'virtual frescoes' projected on the vaulting and niches by 15 projectors could be irresistible even to sceptics.
ⓐ Via San Domenico 28 ⓣ 011 436 5832 ⓦ www.sindone.it ⓛ 09.00–12.00, 15.00–19.00 ⓝ Bus/Tram: 3, 16. Admission charge

Museo di Antichità (Museum of Antiquity)

The Savoys converted the former orangery of their palace into a venue for displaying collections of artefacts from all the ancient Italian diaspora, which includes much of the Mediterranean region. Especially good exhibits feature ancient Cyprus and the Etruscans. Amid these, it's easy to dismiss finds from the local Piedmont area, but those collections do include material from prehistoric sites and from the elusive Frankish years. Look for the Marengo treasure, discovered in 1928, which includes silver and gold work from the 1st and 2nd centuries AD. ⓐ Via XX Settembre 88/C ⓣ 011 521 1106 ⓦ www.museoantichita.it ⓑ 08.30–19.30 Tues–Sun, closed Mon ⓝ Bus/Tram: 13, 56, 57, 63. Admission charge

RETAIL THERAPY

The little back streets of the Quadrilatero are peppered with small shops; for wearables by young and hopeful designers, head for Via Bonelli. Via Garibaldi is an almost solid kilometre of shops, while Europe's biggest street market is in Piazza della Repubblica. Choose Via Mercanti for fine craftsmanship – bookbinders, chandlers and hand-made paper goods.

Autopsie Vestimentaire Alice Capelli, owner of this little shop, is the sole designer of Autopsie Vestimentaire's beautifully eccentric fashions. Natural fabrics and tailored pieces make it an unusual – and essential – stop. ⓐ Via Bligny 12/D ⓣ 011 433 8881 ⓦ www.autopsievestimentaire.com ⓑ 10.00–19.30 Mon–Sat, closed Sun ⓝ Bus/Tram: 52, 60

Colenghi One of Turin's oldest shops, Colenghi has been making fine candles since the late 1700s. It sells everything from tiny candles for birthday cakes and figurals imitating vegetables to stylish dinner table tapers. ⓐ Piazza Solferino 3 ⓣ 011 562 2550 ⓑ Mon–Sat, closed Sun ⓝ Bus/Tram: 5, 14, 29, 57

Emporio Sicomoro Asian Pot Noodles? Wild pickled Piedmontese chicory? A Japanese smoothie? Emporio Sicomoro has it all, and so much more. Shop here to give your groceries a true international flavour.

ⓐ Via Stampatori 6/B ☎ 011 1950 3061 Ⓦ www.emporiosicomoro.it
🕐 16.00–20.00 Mon, 10.00–13.00, 16.00–20.00 Tues & Wed,
10.00–20.00 Thur–Sat, closed Sun Ⓥ Bus/Tram: 4, 11, 12, 72

Porta Palazzo Europe's largest open-air market sprawls across the
piazza and into neighbouring streets, with stalls piled high in fresh
produce, meats, cheeses, spices, clothes, cooking pots, dishes and
gadgets. On Saturday it morphs into an antiques and second-hand
market, Il Balôn, which on the second Sunday of each month expands

⬤ *Porta Palazzo market is just the place for picnic supplies*

to become Il Gran Balôn. The real treasures go early, and bargaining is expected. Piazza della Repubblica ● 07.30–13.00 Mon–Fri, 07.30–19.30 Sat, 07.30–19.30 second Sun of the month
● Bus/Tram: 3, 15, 19, 50, 51

Rosa Serafino Erboristeria At this shop next door to Al Bicerin, deep glass canisters overflow with herbal remedies. Established in 1875.
● Piazza della Consolata 5 ● 011 436 6710 ● Mon–Sat, closed Sun
● Bus/Tram: 3, 16, 52, 60

Weber A number of contemporary artists began their careers at this gallery; look for tomorrow's greats and the latest art trends.
● Via San Tommaso ● 011 812 3519 ● 16.00–19.30 Tues–Sat, closed Sun & Mon ● Bus/Tram: 5, 14, 29, 59, 67

TAKING A BREAK

Part of the reason for wandering the Quadrilatero is to stop in its little side-street cafés and wine bars – whether you're feeling peckish or your feet just need a break from pounding the pavement. Between Via Garibaldi and Via Guilio, every third doorway seems to lead to food and drink. Small plates of snacks and light lunches are best found in these bars and cafés; most restaurants don't serve anything less than a full meal. Around midday, tiny cafés on the east side of Piazza della Repubblica serve cheap pizza and other foods as the market winds down.

Km5 (para beber y comer) £ ❶ Red walls, stencils of bucking broncos, awesome music and a heaving crowd make this spot one of the most energetic in the area. ● Via San Domenico 14–16 ● 011 431 0032
● 18.00–03.00 Tues–Sun, closed Mon ● Bus/Tram: 4, 11, 12, 72

⬧ *The Quadrilatero's tiny streets are stuffed with fantastic restaurants*

Olsen £ ❷ Just off Via Garibaldi, this little bakery/café is well known for inexpensive lunches, which accounts for it being full most of the time. Stop by when it's quieter for a pastry. ⓐ Via Sant'Agostino 4 ① 011 436 1573 ⓛ 08.00–18.30 Mon–Sat, 11.30–18.00 Sun Ⓝ Bus/Tram: 4, 11, 12, 72

San Tommaso 10 £ ❸ Serious coffee drinkers head here, where Luigi Lavazza started his empire and the family has been roasting beans for more than a century. Not surprisingly, the coffee menu is extensive. ⓐ San Tommaso 10 ① 011 534 201 ⓛ Mon–Sat, closed Sun Ⓝ Bus/Tram: 5, 14, 29, 50, 59, 67

Al Bicerin ££ ❹ Choose the drink it's named for – *bicerin*: equal parts espresso, hot chocolate and cream – and enjoy it outside if the weather cooperates. The pastries are excellent. ⓐ Piazza della Consolata 5 ① 011 436 9325 ⓦ www.*bicerin*.it ⓛ 08.30–19.30 Mon, Tues, Thur &Fri, 08.30–12.30, 15.30–19.30 Sat & Sun, closed Wed Ⓝ Bus/Tram: 3, 16, 52, 60

Hafa ££ ❺ Laze on plush cushions and low couches outside of Hafa, the Quadrilatero's trendiest North African café. Stop in for mint tea or an *aperitivo* and snack on plates of falafel, cheese and delicious olives. ⓐ Via Santa Chiara 18/A ① 011 436 2899 ⓦ www.hafa.it ⓛ 20.00–02.00 Mon, 12.00–02.00 Tues–Sun Ⓝ Bus/Tram: 3, 16 ① closest stop is at the west end of Piazza della Repubblica

La Taverna di Guitti ££ ❻ Also just off Via Garibaldi, this taverna serves a plate of starters that is an ample lunch; if you're hungrier, order a hearty plate of house-made tagliolini. ⓐ Via San Dalmazzo 1

☎ 011 533 164 **🕐** 12.30–14.30, 19.30–22.30 Mon–Fri, 19.30–22.30 Sat, closed Sun **Ⓝ** Bus/Tram: 4, 11, 12, 72

AFTER DARK

The Quadrilatero's side-street wine bars and *trattorie* begin to liven up around 19.00, as the Turinese drift in for their evening ritual – the *aperitivo*. Plates of small bites and starters appear on tables with the drinks, and for many locals, replace dinner entirely. Music, occasionally live, adds to the atmosphere. To really fit in, move from one to the next, sampling the food at each. North of these streets is the city's hottest late-night scene, Docks Dora, in the old warehouses near the Dora river.

RESTAURANTS

Brek Ristoranti £ ❼ A quick glance through the glass wall tells you this place is different: fresh fruit and vegetables are everywhere, and the entire kitchen is visible. Take a tray and select your own meal – cooked before your eyes – and pay according to serving size.
ⓐ Piazza Solferino **☎** 011 545 424 **🕐** 11.30–15.00, 18.00–22.30
Ⓝ Bus/Tram: 5, 14, 29, 50, 57

Cook and the City £–££ ❽ Bright colours and quirky furniture decorate this Slow Food café. Whether for an *aperitivo* (the snacks are delicious) or dinner, definitely drop in to check out the action. **ⓐ** Piazza Emanuele Filiberto 3/A **☎** 011 067 3585
🅦 www.cookandthecity.com **🕐** 18.30–late **Ⓝ** Bus/Tram: 3, 16
ⓘ closest stop is at the west end of Piazza della Repubblica

Mille Vigne £–££ ❾ Mille Vigne's garden, with its enchanting fairy lights and swish décor, is one of the most magical places in the Quadrilatero. Stop in for a three-course dinner (€20), or let staff in the adjoining shop advise you on the purchase of a bottle of local wine. ⓐ Via Botero 7/A ❶ Restaurant 011 517 8378, Shop 011 381 9637 ⓦ www.millevignetorino.it ❶ Restaurant 12.30–15.00 Mon, 12.30–15.00, 20.00–23.00 Tues–Fri, 20.00–23.00 Sat & Sun, Shop 10.30–14.00, 15.30–20.00 Mon–Sat, closed Sun ❶ Bus/Tram: 4, 11, 12, 72

Oryza £–££ ❿ Northern Italians eat nearly as much rice as pasta – and it's worth stopping by Oryza to try an eclectic variety of rice recipes, including 13 types of risotto. ⓐ Via Bertola 57 ❶ 011 513 0574 ⓦ www.oryzariso.it ❶ 12.30–14.30 Tues–Fri, 19.45–late Tues–Sun, closed Mon ❶ Bus/Tram: 5, 14, 29, 57

Ristorante Tre Galline £–££ ⓫ Hit one of the most popular restaurants in Turin for some classic Piedmontese fare, such as braised ox, or veal with tuna sauce. ⓐ Via Bellezia 37 ❶ 011 436 6553 ❶ 19.45–23.00 Mon–Sat, closed Sun ❶ Bus/Tram: 3, 16 ❶ closest stop is at the west end of Piazza della Repubblica

Osteria Arcano Matto ££ ⓬ The location of this wine bar/restaurant couldn't be any better, halfway between *piazze* Solferino and Castello. The menu is upmarket and innovative, but not overpriced; look for the daily special. ⓐ Via Pietro Micca 17 ❶ 011 547 953 ⓦ www.arcanomatto.com ❶ 12.00–14.30, 18.00–01.00 ❶ Bus/Tram: 5, 14, 29, 57 or any for Piazza Castello

---

❶ *Order an* aperitivo *and savour the free snacks*

Vintage 1997 ££–£££ Contemporary atmosphere and a chance to sample dishes from Italy's various regions make this chic restaurant a good respite from the same-old. As you might've guessed from the name, the wine list is extensive.
ⓐ Piazza Solferino 16/H ⓣ 011 535 948 ⓦ www.vintage1997.com
ⓛ 12.30–14.30, 19.30–23.00 Mon–Fri, 19.30–23.00 Sat, closed Sun
ⓝ Bus/Tram: 5, 14, 29, 57

CINEMAS & THEATRES

Café Procope Under the Teatro Juvarra, the café stages its own shows and concerts, and is also a pleasant place for a drink.
ⓐ Via Juvarra 15 ⓣ 011 540 675 ⓦ www.masjuvarra.it
ⓝ Bus/Tram: 10, 13, 15, 16, 55, 56, 61, 68

Teatro Alfieri One of Italy's best-known theatres, the Alfieri stages major plays and comedies. Two additional theatres for cinema have been added, both of which show primarily art films.
ⓐ Piazza Solferino 4 ⓣ 011 562 3800 ⓦ www.torinospettacoli.it
ⓝ Bus/Tram: 5, 14, 29, 57

Teatro Gianduja The tiny theatre, part of the marionette museum, is where the puppets perform. Most productions are for all ages with some specifically for children. ⓐ Via Santa Teresa 5 ⓣ 011 530 238
ⓝ Bus/Tram: 1, 4, 9, 11, 12, 15, 18, 51, 55, 56, 67, 68, 72

Teatro Juvarra Located near Piazza Statuto, the Juvarra is dedicated to avant-garde theatre, and has a reputation for multimedia, new technologies and experimental productions.
ⓐ Via Juvarra 15 ⓣ 011 540 675 ⓦ www.masjuvarra.it
ⓝ Bus/Tram: 10, 13, 15, 16, 55, 56, 61, 68

CLUBS, BARS & DISCOS

Arancia di Mezzanotte Instead of the usual plate of snacks on the table, this trendy spot serves a truly outstanding personal buffet with your *aperitivo*. ❸ Piazza Emanuele Filiberto 11/I ❶ 011 521 1138 Ⓦ www.aranciadimezzanotte.it Ⓛ 18.00–01.00 Ⓝ Bus/Tram: 3, 16 ❶ closest stop is at the west end of Piazza della Repubblica

Azimut Styled after a New York loft, Azimut has two different floors offering a choice of music, décor and ambience. Check the schedule in advance – the local live music is often fantastic. ❸ Via Modena 55 ❶ 011 232 458 Ⓛ Wed–Sat, closed Sun–Tues Ⓝ Bus/Tram: 18, 27, 57

Folkclub West of the Quadrilatero (and too late for the buses), the taxi ride is worth it for world music and jazz, often with international artists. The club was originally created in order to preserve and continue to support folk music traditions. ❸ Via Perrone 3/B ❶ 011 537 636 Ⓦ www.folkclub.it Ⓛ Concerts and events vary; check the website in advance

Fusion Café One of the trendiest clubs in one of Turin's trendiest neighbourhoods, Fusion Café blends cutting-edge music, contemporary art exhibitions and divine drinks with a down-to-earth crowd. ❸ Via Sant'Agostino 17 ❶ 011 436 5022 Ⓝ Bus/Tram: 4, 11, 12, 72

Tre Galli Vineria An achingly cool wine bar and restaurant that's teeming on most nights. Reserve a table ahead of time, or be prepared to wait a couple of hours to sip from the magnificent wine list. ❸ Via Sant'Agostino 25 ❶ 011 521 6027 Ⓛ 12.00–14.30, 18.00–02.00 Mon–Sat, closed Sun Ⓝ Bus/Tram: 3, 16 ❶ closest stop is at the west end of Piazza della Repubblica

Along the Po

The River Po tiptoes softly past Turin, a lazy waterway for paddleboats and sightseeing boats, spanned by graceful bridges and lined by grassy parkland and waterside restaurants. Via Po, which sweeps grandly from the Palazzo Reale complex, ends just as dramatically at the river, in Piazza Vittoria Veneto. The habitués of the cafés under its porticoes are university students and expats. The opposite bank of the river rises into the rarefied atmosphere of Borgo Po, its art nouveau villas half hidden in their private parks. Above, a pair of churches offer views of the city from their terraces.

SIGHTS & ATTRACTIONS

If the Savoy centre is characterised by its baroque palaces and the Quadrilatero by its architectural diversity, the neighbourhoods along the Po claim the city's top architectural surprises – or, rather, oddities. The Mole rises head and shoulders above the city like a spiked army helmet, bars and clubs hide under street support arches by the river, a faux medieval village springs from the riverbank and a posh restaurant perches on a rooftop auto test track.

Basilica di Superga

Built as a votive offering following the city's deliverance from the 1706 siege by the French, the church is considered architect Filippo Juvarra's masterpiece. Below (the stairs are to the left of the entrance) are the Savoy tombs and off the cloister is a memorial to the Turinese football team, who were killed in a plane crash here in 1949. ⓐ Strada della Basilica di Superga 73 ⓣ 011 899 7456 ⓦ www.basilicadisuperga.com ⓛ 09.00–12.00, 15.00–17.00 Mon–Fri,

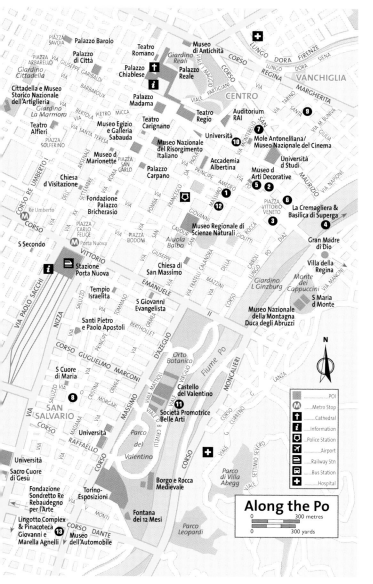

09.00–12.45, 15.00–17.45 Sat & Sun, Oct–Mar; 09.00–12.00, 15.00–18.00 Mon–Fri, 09.00–12.45, 15.00–18.45 Sat & Sun, Apr–Sept, Mass 10.00 Mon–Sat, 10.00, 11.00, 12.00, 17.00 Sun, Oct–Mar; 10.00, 11.00, 12.00, 18.00, Apr–Sept 🚊 Bus/Tram: 15, 61 to the Sassi–Superga Railway (La Cremagliera)

Borgo Medievale

Whenever someone who has never been to Turin suggests that it's a grim industrial city, tell them about Borgo Medievale – living proof that Turin has a sense of humour. This enclave of shops and public buildings appears to be a somewhat over-restored part of the medieval city, but in fact it was built about 400 years too late. Carefully constructed using old techniques and replicating existing architecture and decoration of the period from the surrounding region, the whole village was part of the 1884 Exposition. Entrance is free, and inside are shops, craftsmen (including an armour repair shop in case yours is dented) and buildings to wander among. 🚩 Viale Virgilio, Parco del Valentino, Corso Massimo D'Azeglio 📞 011 433 1701 🌐 www.borgomedievaletorino.it 🕐 09.00–20.00 Apr–Oct; 9.00–19.00 Nov–Mar 🚊 Bus/Tram: 9, 16, 34, 67

Castello del Valentino (Valentino Castle)

Bought by the Savoys in 1564, not long after it was built, the castle served as a residence until it became home to the university's Department of Architecture. Although it's officially not open to the public, you can usually just walk in and look around. 🚩 Parco del Valentino, Corso Massimo D'Azeglio 🚊 Bus/Tram: 9, 16, 34, 67

Chiesa di San Massimo (Church of St Maximus)

Built in the 1840s, when this section of the city was being developed, this neoclassical church is of particular interest to musicians, who

ROYAL PALACES

Within a short bus ride of the city centre, several of the Savoy royal palaces are open for tours. All are included in the Torino Card (see page 52).

Castello della Mandria & Parco Regionale La Mandria

The castle is actually a collection of 25 structures that belonged to the Savoy kings. The apartments of Borgo Castello, the principal royal residence, can be seen on a guided tour. On the park grounds are old farmsteads, such as the Cascina Comba and the Cascina Vittoria. Look for the chapel of San Giuliano, which dates from 1263. Bicycling and horse riding are available.
ⓐ Via Carlo Emanuele II 256, Venaria Reale ❶ 011 499 3311
ⓦ www.parks.it ❶ 08.00–20.00 Mar–Sept, earlier closing rest of the year ❷ Bus: 72 from Piazza Castello to Venaria (entrance 2.5 km)

Castello di Rivolli

It was Duke Emanuele Filiberto who first turned this castle into a royal residence. Destroyed by fire by French troops in 1693, it was repaired under the architects Michelangelo Garove and Filippo Juvarra, only to fall into disuse after the Napoleonic era. Recent renovations have restored much of its 18th-century magnificence, while also creating the Museo d'Arte Contemporanea, which it now houses.
ⓐ Piazza Malfada di Savoia, Rivoli (13 km (8 miles) west of Turin) ❶ 011 956 522 ⓦ www.castellodirivoli.org
❶ 10.00–17.00 Tues–Thur, 10.00–21.00 Fri–Sun, closed Mon

Bus: 36 to end, weekend shuttle from Piazza Castello. Admission charge

Palazzina di Caccia di Stupinigi

This magnificent baroque palace was begun in 1729 on the orders of Carlo Amadeo II and under the direction of Filippo Juvarra. The heavily ornamented rooms were once occupied by Napoleon. It is now home to the Museo di Arte e Ammobiliamento (Museum of Art & Furniture), as well as extraordinary gardens. Note that the palace is closed until late 2008. Piazza Principe Amadeo 7, Stupingi, Nichelino 011 358 1220 www.mauriziano.it 10.00–17.00 Tues–Sun, closed Mon Bus: 41

Reggia di Venaria Reale

Begun in 1659 as a palace with supporting village, its size is often compared to Versailles. The great architects Castellamonte, Garove, Juvarra and Alfiere all contributed to its design and construction. Long neglected, it is in the process of restoration. Piazza della Repubblica 4, Venaria Reale 011 562 3530 www.reggiavenariareale.it 09.00–11.30, 14.30–19.00 Tues, Thurs, Sat & Sun, closed Mon, Wed & Fri Bus: 72, 77 to Venaria Reale

will want to see and hear the organ. Built by one of the most prominent organ-makers of his day, Carlo Bossi, this enormous instrument of more than 3,000 pipes won the gold medal at the 1884 Italian Exposition, and was a favourite of both Berlioz and Mendelssohn. In the baptistry,

Legnanino's 1707 altarpiece depicting the Nativity of the Virgin predates the church by more than a century; the striking large stained-glass window was created in 1949. ❸ Via Mazzini 29 (corner of Via Massimo) ❶ 011 812 6703 ❹ 08.00–12.00, 16.00–19.30 Mon–Fri, 08.00–12.30, 17.45–19.30 Sat & Sun, Mass 18.30 Mon–Sat, 08.30, 10.30, 11.30, 18.30 Sun ❻ Bus/Tram: 18, 61, 63

La Cremagliera

Use the rack railway to access the basilica or the walking trails that weave through the natural park at the top, or just for the ride and the views of Turin and the Alps. ❸ Sassi ❶ 011 576 4733 ❻ www.comune.torino.it ❹ 09.00–12.00, 14.00–20.00 Mon, Wed–Fri, 09.00–20.00 Sat & Sun, leaving Sassi on the hour and Superga on the half hour ❻ Bus/Tram: 15, 60

Lingotto complex

In 1983 Renzo Piano was commissioned to transform FIAT's first American-style assembly-line plant, built in 1923, into a showpiece – and, by the time it reopened in 2002, he had certainly succeeded. Bold designs and state-of-the-art techno features – window blinds that follow the sun, glass roofs that slide into place over courtyard cafés in case of rain – turned the redundant factory into 90 shops, two hotels, an art museum and a rooftop restaurant you can drive to. The rooftop test track with Alpine views is now a running and walking track for hotel guests. FIAT enthusiasts should stop to see the first FIAT factory at 102 Corso Dante, just past Parco del Valentino, a 1904–06 *Stile Liberty* (art nouveau) building designed by Alfredo Premoli. ❸ Via Nizza 280 ❻ www.lingottofiere.it ❹ Otto Gallery (shopping) 12.00–22.00 Mon, 10.00–22.00 Tues–Sun ❻ Bus/Tram: 1, 18, 35

Mole Antonelliana

Symbol of the city, and its best viewpoint if you've a head for heights, the Mole has a history that's as strange as its architecture. Its name translates to Antonelli's Heap, for Alessandro Antonelli, its architect. It began life as a synagogue, or at least it was intended as one. But it became such an expensive project that the congregation abandoned it to the city, which then decided it would be a monument to King Vittorio Emanuele II instead. But the building itself didn't have a permanent use until it finally became the site of the Museum of Cinema (see page 105), a fitting use for this larger-than-life heap. If you have a head (and the stomach!) for heights, take the glass lift to the top on a clear day for a breathtaking view of the Alps and the city. ⓐ Via Montebello 20 ⓘ 011 813 8560 ⓛ 10.00–20.00 Tues–Fri, 10.00–23.00 Sat, 10.00–20.00 Sun, closed Mon ⓝ Bus/Tram: 13, 15, 16, 55, 56, 68. Admission/lift charge

I Murazzi

The 19th-century architects who designed the sturdy arches to support the streets among the Po embankment might be surprised to see them on a summer Saturday night. Under the arcades between Ponto Umberto and Ponto Vittorio Emanuele, it's one long block party, as revellers drift from bar to bar and club to club. In colder seasons the action moves elsewhere, but in summer this is definitely the place to be. ⓝ Bus/Tram: 13, 15, 16, 30, 53, 55, 56, 61

Orto Botanico (Botanic Gardens)

Begun as a source of medicinal plants, this small garden within Parco del Valentino contains rare and alpine plants and a herbarium. ⓐ Viale

● *Turin's most striking building, the Mole Antonelliana*

Mattioli 25 011 670 5985 www.bioveg.unito.it 09.00–13.00, 15.00–19.00 Sat & Sun, closed Mon–Fri Bus/Tram: 9, 16, 34, 67. Admission charge

Parco del Valentino

The green band of parkland stretches for nearly a mile along the Po from Ponte Umberto to Ponte Isabella, much of it facing woodlands on the opposite bank and giving the river a rural look in the midst of the city. Vehicle-free Viale Virgilio runs near the river the entire length of the park, a favourite place for walkers, cyclists and joggers in the daytime. It leads to sites within the park, an excursion boat landing and several waterside restaurants. Corso Vittorio Emanuele, Corso Massimo D'Azeglio Bus/Tram: 9, 16, 34 67

Piazza Vittorio Veneto

On reaching the river, arcaded Via Po ends in a flourish. Piazza Vittorio Veneto's impressive size and portico-surrounded perimeter are so perfectly designed that they disguise the 12 m (35ft) difference in street level from one side to the other. In the winter cafés and restaurants hide under the arcades; in summer they overflow into the pedestrianised areas. Bus/Tram: 13, 15, 16, 55, 56, 61

River boat trips along the Po: Valentina & Valentino

Modern glass-enclosed boats, the Valentino and Valentina, cruise from the Borgo Medievale downstream to the Murazzi or upstream as far as Moncalieri, for views of the city and river landscapes. Parco del Valentino, Corso Massimo D'Azeglio 011 546 4733, Reservations 011 744 892 www.comune.torino.it Departures 15.00, 16.15, 17.45 Sun, mid-Sept–mid–June; 15.00, 16.15, 17.45, 19.00,

● Head to the Basilica di Superga to admire amazing Alpine vistas

21.30, 22.45 (last two trips by reservation only) Tues–Sat, 10.30 Sun, mid-June–mid-Sept ● Bus/Tram: 13, 15, 16, 30, 53, 55, 56, 61, 70

Rocca Medievale

Also built for the Exposition, the castle is a convincing replica of those that line the Val d'Aosta, including their frescoes, faithfully reproduced on the walls. Admission is charged for a tour of the building, which even has period sound effects. ● Viale Virgilio, Parco del Valentino, Corso Massimo D'Azeglio ● 011 433 1701 ● www.borgomedievaletorino.it ● 09.00–19.00 Tues–Sun, closed Mon ● Bus/Tram: 9, 16, 34, 67. Admission charge

Villa della Regina

Constructed in 1615 and further enhanced by Princess Ludovica in the late 17th century, the Villa della Regina is a mix of elegant sculptures, gardens and fountains. The Villa is under restoration until early 2008 – call ahead to book a visit. ❸ Strada Santa Margherita 79 ❶ 011 564 1778 Ⓦ www.artito.arti.beniculturali.it Ⓝ Bus/Tram: 13, 55, 56, 66

CULTURE

Although this part of Turin is not as packed with museums as the area around the Savoy palace, it has its fair share, including the Cinema Museum and one of Europe's best collections of classic and antique cars.

Fondazione Sandretto Re Rebaudengo

One of the most important contemporary art museums in Italy, the Fondazione Sandretto is a little off the beaten track, but well worth the effort. Check out the oh-so-cool Ristorante Spazio, also on site. ❸ Via Modane 16 ❶ 011 379 7600 Ⓦ www.fondsrr.org Ⓛ 12.00–20.00 Tues, Wed & Fri–Sun, 12.00–23.00 Thur, closed Mon Ⓝ Bus/Tram: 10, 16, 42, 58, 64, 66

Museo dell'Automobile (Car Museum)

The collection of about 170 vehicles is one of the largest in the world, and housed in a 1960s building that is itself a splendid example of modern architecture. The cars date from the very earliest motor vehicles, designed and built in the mid-1800s. Italian makes predominate the collections, with an even dozen Alfa Romeos, eight Ferraris, 27 FIATs (this is their home, after all), three Maseratis, four Isotta Fraschinis and a couple of Bugattis. But other significant makes and places are represented, too, including such makes as Packard, Mercedes Benz, Rolls-Royce, Jaguar and Stanley Steamer. Along with road models are racing cars and rare examples of celebrity cars used in movies. Note that the museum will reopen late 2008 after restoration. ⓐ Corso Unità d'Italia 40 ⓣ 011 677 666 ⓦ www.museoauto.it ⓛ 10.00–18.30 Tues–Sun, closed Mon ⓝ Bus/Tram: 1, 18, 34, 35, 45, 74. Admission charge

Museo Nazionale del Cinema (Cinema Museum)

Beginning with the earliest work of the Lumière brothers, this state-of-the-art spectacle dazzles with themed exhibits on various genres, the technical process, sets, personalities, film stars and every other facet of the industry. Watch film classics in a variety of theatre settings, including a heart-shaped bed (for love stories, of course). Props, sets and stage models round out an experience that will please any film fan (see Mole Antonelliana, page 100). ⓐ Via Montebello 20 ⓣ 011 813 8560 ⓦ www.museonazionaledelcinema.org ⓛ 10.00–20.00 Tues–Fri, 10.00–23.00 Sat, 10.00–20.00 Sun, closed Mon ⓝ Bus/Tram: 13, 15, 16, 55, 56, 68. Admission/lift charge

Museo Nazionale della Montagna (Mountain Museum)

Exhibits in this surprisingly complete museum include mountain traditions, art, geology, natural history, alpine plants and wildlife, as well as the development of mountaineering sports (including climbing and skiing), in the Alps and other ranges. Interesting as this may be, if the day is clear, many people give these exhibits a brief glance on their way to the observation level. Here the Alps themselves spread before you in a magnificent panorama. Well worth the climb up the Capuchins' Mountain. ⓐ Via Giardino 39 – Monte dei Cappuccini ⓣ 011 660 4104 ⓦ www.museomontagna.org ⓛ 09.00–19.00 Tues–Sun, closed Mon ⓝ Bus: 53. Admission charge

Museo Regionale di Scienze Naturali (Museum of Natural Sciences)

Located in a former 17th-century hospital, Turin's Museum of Natural Sciences hosts a wide range of exhibitions, as well as offering a specialist library, which is open to the public. Ⓐ Via Giolitti 36 Ⓣ 011 432 6354 Ⓦ www.regione.piemonte.it Ⓛ 10.00–19.00 Wed–Mon, closed Tues Ⓜ Bus/Tram: 13, 18, 56, 61, 68. Admission charge

Pinacoteca Giovanni & Marella Agnelli
(Giovanni & Marella Agnelli Art Gallery)

The selections from Giovanni and Marella Agnelli's art collection – one of Italy's most significant and of which this is but a small fraction – are shown in a purpose-built gallery designed by Renzo Piano. The Turinese call it *lo scrigno* (the casket) for its peculiar shape, appended onto the Lingotto. The few (about two dozen) works shown include some outstanding ones, by Tiepolo, Manet, Renoir, Matisse and Modigliani, along with six Venetian scenes by Canaletto. Ⓐ Via Nizza 262

🔺 *Castello di Rivolli showing off its magnificence by night*

☎ 011 006 2713 ⓦ www.pinacoteca-agnelli.it 🕐 09.00–19.00 Tues–Sun, closed Mon 🚌 Bus/Tram: 1, 18, 35. Admission charge

RETAIL THERAPY

Between the pricey big-name shops of the Via Roma and the equally pricey boutiques of the Borgo Po is the university, bringing reason to the prices, but wild abandon to the styles. Shop under the arcades of Via Po for funky clothes (and second-hand books in all languages) and along trendy (and correspondingly more expensive) Via Mazzini for higher fashion, sometimes cut-price from designers.

Creativity Original housewares and suchlike, from top designers as well as emerging craftsmen. 🅰 Via Mazzini 29 ☎ 011 817 7864 🕐 15.30–19.30 Mon, 10.00–13.00, 15.30–19.30 Tues, Wed, Fri & Sat; 10.00–19.30 Thur, closed Sun 🚌 Bus/Tram: 18, 61, 68

Eataly For the aspiring chef or simply those passionate about food, be sure to plan a lazy afternoon, snacking and shopping at the giant Eataly complex (see page 13). 🅰 Via Nizza 230, Torino Lingotto ☎ 011 1950 6811 ⓦ www.eatalytorino.it 🕐 10.00–22.00 Tues–Sun, closed Mon 🚌 Bus/Tram: 1, 18, 35

Galleria Maze Lively venue to see the work of young artists without the pomp of the more establishment galleries. 🅰 Via Mazzini 40 ☎ 011 815 4145 ⓦ www.galleriamaze.it 🕐 10.30–19.30 Mon–Fri, 15.00–20.00 Sat, closed Sun 🚌 Bus/Tram: 18, 61

Gioielli da Calzare If clothes can be radical and classic all at once, this shop pulls it off, with the kind of shoes and accessories that

chic Via Mazzini shoppers have come to expect. ❷ Via Mazzini 7/F
(at Carlo Alberto) ☏ 011 546 592 ⓦ www.gioiellidacalzare.it
🕐 15.30–19.30 Mon, 10.30–13.30, 15.30–19.30 Tues, Wed, Fri & Sat,
10.30–19.30 Thur, closed Sun ⓝ Bus/Tram: 49, 15, 63

Giulebbe Pack an elegant picnic here and head for the riverbank at
Parco del Valentino. No bargains, but top-quality food gifts from the
length of Italy. ❷ Via della Rocca 39 (just off Via Mazzini) ☏ 011 882 855
🕐 Mon–Sat, closed Sun ⓝ Bus/Tram: 16, 52

Scout This places tries just a little too hard to be on the cutting edge
of *la moda*, but a good place to stay ahead of the pack nonetheless.
❷ Via Lagrange 22 ☏ 011 546 589 🕐 15.00–19.00 Mon, 10.30–19.30
Tues–Fri, 10.00–13.00, 15.00–19.30 Sat, closed Sun ⓝ Bus/Tram: 4, 11,
12, 13, 15, 18, 27, 51, 55, 56, 57, 63, 72

TAKING A BREAK

The arcades of Piazza Victoria Veneto and Via Po scarcely conceal the
multitude of cafés that provide a second home to university students.
Other small cafés are scattered along the streets near the Po, so you're
never far from a place for an espresso or a Negroni.

Amantes £ ❶ A combined art gallery and *aperitivo* bar, Amantes is
a pleasant evening option, with great ambience and relaxing music.
❷ Via Principe Amadeo 38/A ☏ 011 817 2427 ⓦ www.arteca.org
🕐 18.00–01.30 Mon–Sat, closed Sun ⓝ Bus/Tram: 13, 15, 16, 30, 53, 55, 61

Caffè Elena £ ❷ Students mix with literary types at this historical
café, which was a favourite of Nietzsche. It's one of the many that

⬤ *An oasis of calm from Turin's daytime bustle*

spill out into the piazza in good weather. ⓐ Piazza Vittorio Veneto 5
ⓣ 011 812 3341 ⓛ 08.30–23.00 Sun–Tues & Thur, 08.30–01.00 Fri & Sat
ⓦ Bus/Tram: 13, 15, 16, 30, 53, 55, 61

La Drogheria £ ❸ Go for an aperitif in the late afternoon or for lunch.
The *aperitivo* hour is a sacred institution here, accompanied by tasty
snacks that attract a fashionable youngish set every afternoon.
Check out the eclectic selection of tables. ⓐ Piazza Vittorio Veneto 18
ⓣ 011 812 2414 ⓛ 10.00–02.00 Sun–Thurs, 10.00–03.00 Fri & Sat
ⓦ Bus/Tram: 13, 15, 16, 30, 53, 55, 61

Cantine Risso £–££ ❹ Lunches here are excellent, especially the
exquisite salads in the summertime – be sure to grab a seat in the
sun-dappled courtyard. Sample local wines at the bar in the evening.
ⓐ Corso Casale 79 ⓣ 011 819 5531 ⓛ 12.00–15.00, 19.30–02.00 Mon–Fri,
19.30–02.00 Sat & Sun ⓦ Bus/Tram: 13, 51, 61

Cremeria Ghigo ££ ❺ Famous since the Savoys nibbled their
Ghigo chocolates, Ghigo is busy from breakfast into the tiny hours.
The speciality is anything cream-filled or cream-topped. ⓐ Via Po 52
ⓣ 011 887 017 ⓛ 07.30–20.00 Mon–Sat, 07.30–13.30 Sun ⓦ Bus/Tram:
13, 15, 16, 30, 53, 55, 61

Vinicola Al Sorji ££ ❻ Aperitivi, over 500 types of wine and a few
well-prepared meal options make this wine bar, just a few steps from
Piazza Vittorio Veneto, ever popular. ⓐ Via Matteo Pescatore 10/C
ⓣ 011 835 667 ⓦ www.alsorij.it ⓛ 18.00–02.00 Mon–Sat, closed Sun
ⓦ Bus/Tram: 13, 15, 16, 30, 53, 55, 61

AFTER DARK

The evening begins with an aperitif or two in the cafés of Piazza Vittorio Veneto (where you might meet Subsonica in Caffè Elena – their studio is just around the corner). The late-night buzz increases as you move towards the river, reaching a crescendo under the arches built to support the riverside streets. The Murazzi, which opens onto the river, is the summer meeting point for clubbers, who jump from one place to another, and for those who prefer to hear the music beat from the outside. The only things outnumbering the glasses of wine consumed here on a summer evening are the mosquitoes, so wear insect repellant with your Euro-casual gear.

RESTAURANTS

AL 24 £–££ ❼ Near the Mole Antonelliana, this small eatery mixes Tuscan influences into its Piemontese cuisine. Look for truffle specials in season. ⓐ Via Montebello 24 ❶ 011 812 2981 ⓛ Daily, closed lunch Mon–Tues & late June–mid-July ⓝ Bus/Tram: 13, 15, 16, 55, 56, 61, 68

Dai Saletta £–££ ❽ A short walk from Parco del Valentino, this small neighbourhood favourite serves local dishes with updated touches. Don't miss the *trifulin* (truffle ravioli) or the *arrosto alla crema di nocciole* (roasted veal in a hazelnut cream sauce). ⓐ Via Belfiore 37 ❶ 011 668 7867 ⓛ 12.30–14.30, 20.00–20.30 Mon–Sat, closed Sun ⓝ Bus/Tram: 9, 16, 52

Gaia Scienza £–££ ❾ Piedmont traditions mix with a few inventive dishes in this cosy *osteria*. Along with the expected *bagna cauda* and *fritto misto piemontese* (with meat) is the house speciality,

penne alla zarina (pasta with smoked salmon, roe and vodka).
ⓐ Via Guastalla 22 (between Corso Regina and Corso San Maurizio)
ⓣ 011 812 3821 ⓒ 20.30–24.00 Mon–Sat, closed Sun ⓝ Bus/Tram: 13, 15, 16, 55, 56, 61, 68

Sotto la Mole £–££ ⑩ Piedmont meets the rest of Italy in the kitchen underneath the Mole Antonelliana. Recently named a Slow Food favourite, the dining room is lively and the food tasty, plentiful and well-priced. ⓐ Via Montebello 9 ⓣ 011 817 9398 ⓒ 19.30–23.00 Thur–Tues, closed Wed ⓝ Bus/Tram: 13, 15, 16, 55, 56, 61, 68

L'Idrovolante ££ ⑪ The waterside setting within a leafy park is reason enough to eat here, but the menu trumps that with dishes such as grilled swordfish with sun-dried tomatoes and capers or grilled veal with taleggio, asparagus and fresh marjoram. Traditional country dinner on Sundays. ⓐ Viale Virgilio 105, Parco del Valentino ⓣ 011 668 7602 ⓦ www.ristorranteidrovolante.com ⓒ 12.00–14.30, 19.30–23.00 Tues–Sun, closed Mon ⓝ Bus/Tram: 9, 16, 34, 67

Il Punto Verde ££ ⑫ Any Italian restaurant will offer a fair few veggie dishes, but for true vegetarian fare, head to Il Punto Verde. Be sure to try the antipasti buffet and the grilled seitan with courgettes. ⓐ Via San Massimo 17 ⓣ 011 885 543 ⓦ www.il-punto-verde.it ⓒ 12.30–14.30, 19.30–22.30 Mon–Fri, 19.30–22.30 Sat, closed Sun & Aug ⓝ Bus/Tram: 18, 61

La Pista £££ ⑬ The one reason for driving a car in the city would be to arrive at this rooftop restaurant in the Lingotto building by driving up the spiral ramp (alternatively, you can get here by taxi!). Save room for a dessert, all of which are served on FIAT engine pieces.

🅐 Lingotto Building, Via Nizza 280 ☎ 011 631 3523 🕐 12.30–15.00, 19.30–23.00 Wed–Mon, closed Tues 🚍 Bus/Tram: 1, 18, 35

THEATRES & MUSIC

Auditorium Giovanni Agnelli Classical performances, particularly chamber music, is the forte of this companion to the Agnelli family's art gallery, in the same complex. 🅐 Via Nizza 262, Lingotto ☎ 011 664 0458 🌐 www.expo2000.it 🚍 Bus/Tram: 1, 18, 35

🔺 *Even the Museum of Cinema has an atmospheric bar*

Teatro Colosseo Toast the annual showing of the *Rocky Horror Show* at this eclectic theatre, which also features popular musicals, stage plays and stand-up routines. ⓐ Via Madama Cristina 71 ⓣ 011 669 8034 ⓦ www.teatrocolosseo.it

CLUBS, BARS & DISCOS

Centralino Club Live rock and DJ sounds fill this underground venue, which is favoured by a very young crowd; Friday is gay night. ⓐ Via delle Rosine 16 ⓣ 011 837 500 ⓛ 24.00–05.00 Tues & Thur, 24.00–06.00 Fri–Sun, closed Mon & Wed, July & Aug ⓝ Bus/Tram: 13, 15, 55, 61

Da Giancarlo One of the best late-night venues on the Murazzi and an all-time favourite with local musicians, Da Giancarlo recently moved to new premises up the road. ⓐ Murazzi del Po ⓣ 011 817 472 ⓛ Tues–Sun, closed Mon ⓝ Bus/Tram: 13, 15, 16, 30, 53, 55, 61

Hiroshima Mon Amour Although it's moved to a new location not far from the Lingotto complex, this club is still a Turinese institution. ⓐ Via Bossoli 83 ⓣ 011 317 6636 ⓦ www.hiroshimamonamour.org ⓛ Thur–Sun, closed Mon–Wed ⓝ Bus/Tram: 1, 18, 35

▶ *Alpine peaks and rambling countryside surround Turin*

The Olympic mountain towns

Until 2006 the Val di Susa, Val del Chisone and neighbouring valleys were ski and summer sports havens known to very few beyond Turin and Milan. The fact that Turin and these valleys hosted the 2006 Winter Games changed all that. Thankfully, what did not change is the spectacular scenery or the basic feel of these little villages, where high-style ski wear and late-night discos blend with wilderness trails and centuries-old mountain traditions.

● *The Italian Alps are a paradise for any skier*

SIGHTS & ATTRACTIONS

Along with skiing and many other winter sports, this region offers summer hiking, mountain biking and alpine rides. A stunning fortress monastery and some Roman sites add to the mix, but the scenery alone is worth hiring a car or hopping on the direct train into the mountains. You can access these valleys on the A32 or the slower S25. To get to the A32 from downtown Turin, follow Corso Regine Margarite.

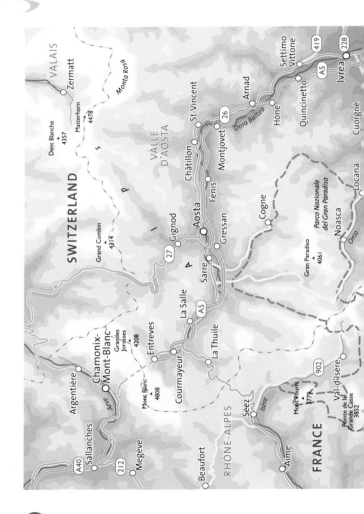

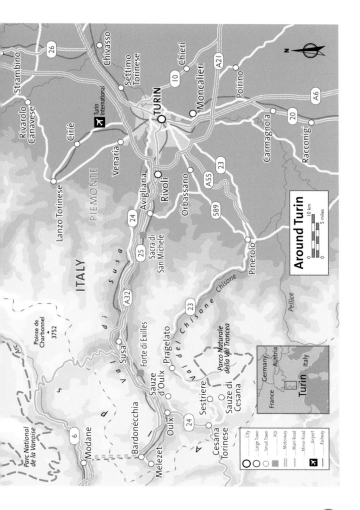

Around Turin

0 10 km
0 5 miles

City
Large Town
Small Town
POI
Motorway
Main Road
Minor Road
Airport
Railway

Strambino
Chivasso
Settimo Torinese
Chieri
Moncalieri
Poirino
Rivarolo Canavese
Rivoli
TURIN
Turin International
Ciriè
Venaria
Carmagnola
Racconigi
Lanzo Torinese
Avigliana
Orbassano
PIEMONTE
ITALY
Sacra di San Michele
Pinerolo
Susa
Val di Susa
Val Chisone
Val Chisone
Pellice
Pointe de Charbonnel
3752
Forte di Exilles
Pragelato
Parc National de la Vanoise
Bardonecchia
Sauze d'Oulx
Sestriere
Parco Naturale della Val Troncea
Sauze di Cesana
Modane
Melezet
Oulx
Cesana Torinese

France
Germany
Austria
Italy
Turin

Bardonecchia

A warren of medieval houses fills the old town of this ski resort snuggled up against the French border and at the foot of massive mountains. A 12 km (7 1/2-mile) tunnel, Traforo del Frejus, bores through the mountain to Mondane, in France. South of town on Colomion (2,100 m/6,500 ft), La Selletta (2,230 m/6,900 ft) and on the flanks of Mt Jefferau (2,807m/8,700 ft) to the east, ski slopes provide the trails that were used for the snowboard, giant slalom, half-pipe and snowboard cross competitions of the 2006 Olympics. When not used for Olympics, the area is known for beginner-friendly trails: 18 trails for intermediate skiers and ten for beginners. Facilities include Nordic trails, ice skating, ice climbing, snow-shoeing and snowmobiling. Ⓦ www.comune.bardonecchia.to.it

Cesana Torinese

The small villages that huddle among the mountain passes include Cesana, the largest, San Sicario and Monte Fraitève. The trip from Oulx to Claviere (S24) follows the valley of the river Dora Riparia into a land of hidden valleys. The fact that many events were held here during the 2006 Olympics led to improvements in the skiing facilities. Ⓦ www.comune.cesana.to.it

Parco Naturale della Val Troncea

Following the Chisone river, the park spreads onto the surrounding hillsides. A variety of attractive walking, hiking and mountain-bike trails are in the park, mapped from easy to difficult. One leads to where copper was mined in the 19th century, until the site and the town were abandoned in the 1920s. The park is home to deer, ibex, boar, wolves, fox, ermine and bird life, and the visitor centre has a small museum with displays on these and on the mining history.

ⓐ Via della Pineta Frazione Rua, Pragelato ⓣ 0122 788 49
ⓦ www.parconaturalevaltroncea.it

Pragelato

Another tiny town, this one is famed for its Nordic skiing. Regularly
groomed ski trails and walking paths head from town into the Parco
Naturale della Val Troncea. Rent mountain bikes at **Il Fouia**, a hotel/bar
in La Rua (ⓣ 0122 78884) or **Pizzeria Il Mulino** in the village of Plan
(ⓣ 0122 78002). The ski jump, built for the men's ski jumping competitions
of the 2006 Olympics and used for the 2005 World Cup, provides for
additional winter sport opportunities. The town also has an indoor
swimming pool.

Sacra di San Michele

The towering monastery dominates its surroundings from the top
of Mount Pirchiriano. Begun in 983, it was the home to a powerful
Benedictine community until it was closed in 1622. While parts of the
complex are in ruins, major portions have been restored. Particularly
impressive are the overpowering entrance façade, the archways at the
entrance to the church and the Grand Staircase of the Dead. At the top
is an archway carved in the 12th century by Master Nicolao, showing
the zodiac and constellations. ⓐ Via Alla Sacra 14, Sant'Ambrogio (near
Avigliana) ⓣ 011 939 130 ⓦ www.sacradisanmichele.com ⓛ 09.30–12.30,
15.00–18.00 Mon–Fri, 09.30–12.00, 14.40–18.30 Sun, closed Sat, mid-Mar–
mid-Oct; 09.30–12.30, 15.00–17.00 Tues–Fri, 09.30–12.00, 14.40–17.00
Sun, closed Mon & Sat, mid-Oct–mid-Mar. Admission charge

Sauze d'Oulx

Three mountain peaks soar above this small resort town, where
pioneer downhill skiers paved the way for the freestyle and men's

and women's mogul competitions of the 2006 Olympics. World Cup and Olympic gold medal slalom skier Piero Gros grew up here. By car, exit the A32 onto S24 at Oulx; it's well signposted from there.
ⓦ www.comune.sauzedoulx.to.it

Sestriere

Another venue for the 2006 Olympics, Sestriere is one of the grand old places of Italian skiing, a legacy of FIAT's Giovanni Agnelli who, in the 1930s, decided to build four cable cars, ski facilities and a pair of hotels at the foot of the mountains. As one of the earliest ski resorts, it has the most facilities and the richest clientele of the Susa-Chisone ski areas, but it's nothing to look at (unless you count people-watching, that is). In addition to skiing, the winter offers bobsledding, heli-skiing and dog sledding – you can even take lessons at **Scuola Italiana Conduttori Cani da Slitta** (ⓣ 012 283 2473). Summer activities include hiking, climbing, mountain biking and golf at Europe's highest course, **Sestrieres Golf Club** (ⓣ 012 279 9411)
ⓦ www.comune.sestriere.to.it

Susa

The Romans may have left Susa in the 4th century AD, but their buildings far outlasted them. Look for the massive gateway, Porta Savoia, built in the 2nd century AD. Both ends are embedded in later buildings, but you'll notice its similarity to Porta Palatina in Turin. Arco Augusto, dating from 9 BC, commemorates a truce with the local Celts. An aqueduct, Terme Graziane, was built toward the end of Roman rule. The Cathedral San Giusto, dating from the 11th century, retains its Romanesque bell tower, as well as later Gothic features and fine carved wooden choir stalls.

THE OLYMPIC MOUNTAIN TOWNS

Val del Chisone

Running between Pinerolo, southwest of Turin, and Sestriere, the valley of the Chisone River cuts through Parco Naturale della Val Troncea and past the ski resort of Pregelato. The fastest way there might be the Corso Regina Margarite to the A32 west to Oulx, then the S24 and S23. The alternative is to follow Via Sacchi, which becomes Corso Federico Turati, to S23 and on to Pinerolo, at the eastern end of the valley. Pinerolo was the site of the curling competitions of the 2006 Winter Olympics. ⓐ Turismo Viale Giolitti, Pinerolo ⓣ 0121 794 003 ⓦ www.montagnedoc.it

CULTURE

The great outdoors and mountain sports are the draw in these towns, but a few interesting museums are worth a stop if you have time. Their opening times tend to be erratic, so it's best to call unless you're already driving right past.

Forte di Exilles

From very early times there has been an important fortress here, protecting the region from invasions from the north. It was so huge and unwieldy, however, that Napoleon ordered it destroyed. Shortly after he gave up his Italian kingdom the fort was rebuilt and has since been restored, now housing a museum of the history and culture of the Alpine region. Access is from the S335 or A32 west of Susa. ⓐ Exilles ⓣ 012 258 270 ⓦ www.cmavs.it ⓛ 10.00–19.00 Tues–Sun, closed Mon, May–Sept; 10.00–14.00 Tues–Sun, closed Mon, Oct, Mar & Apr

Museo Civico Etnografico

The little home-grown museum interprets life in the Alpine valleys through old farm implements and household items. ⓐ Via des Geneys 6, Bardonecchia ⓣ 012 290 2612 ⓛ 15.00–19.00 Mon–Fri, July & Aug; 09.00–12.30, 15.00–19.00 Sat & Sun, also by advance reservation

Museo d'Arte Preistorica

Unique in the scope of its collections – it covers prehistoric rock art throughout Europe – this museum gives a window into prehistoric art from the Neolithic to the Iron Age. ⓐ Viale Giolitti 1, Pinerolo ⓣ 012 179 4382 ⓦ www.cesmap.it

● *Stock up on* gianduoitti, *one type of heavenly Turinese chocolate*

Museo del Costume delle Tradizioni delle Genti Alpine
Glimpse into the lives of the rugged mountain people who have populated these towns for generations, through the clothing and tools used in their daily lives. ● Via San Giovanni, Borgata Rivetta, Pragelato ● 012 278 800 ● 10.00–12.30, 15.00–18.00 Aug, 15.00–18.00 Sat, 10.00–12.30, 15.00–18.00 Sun, closed Mon–Fri, Sept–July. Admission charge

RETAIL THERAPY

The latest skiwear, woodcarvings and local edibles and drinkables are the prime shopping subjects in the region, along with climbing and hiking gear in the summer. Bardonecchia's main street is lined with shops offering hand-made wooden carvings, and in the Cesana Torinese towns look for the herb liqueur, salamis and Toma cheeses that these towns are noted for.

Don't pass through Avigliana without tasting – and stocking up on – *baci al cioccolato* and *Aviglianesi al rhum*, both delectable sweets. Serious resort shoppers should head straight for Sestriere, where shops around the Piazza Fraiteve clothe the very well-heeled and trendy.

TAKING A BREAK

Surprisingly, food at the trailside cafés and snack bars is quite cheap and good, and pizzerias abound for the budget-minded. By late afternoon, skiers have begun to fill the cafés and bars, many of which serve snacks with drinks.

Café Medail £ Pleasant staff, who serve good quick pick-me-ups and drinks. ● Via Stazione 2, Bardonecchia ● 012 299 9844

Italian £ Mega pizzas, cheap prices, friendly atmosphere.
 Via Medail, Bardonecchia

Filanda £–££ At Filanda, the chefs' pizza-twirling antics are as
enjoyable as the finished product.  Via Medail 100, Bardonecchia
 012 299 9780

AFTER DARK

Don't expect a tourist-style club scene in quiet Bardonecchia,
but if you're willing to join in with the local life, ask where the
rock bands Schiffida and Derrymain are playing. Après-ski lasts
most of the night in Sauze d'Oulx, where Via Assietta is lined
with bars and pubs.

Things really heat up in chi-chi Sestriere – if the town were
more attractive, you might mistake it for Courmayeur (or St Moritz)
from the clientele and the bars and cafés around Piazza Fraiteve.
Drinks are expensive, but the snacks are generous.

BARS, CLUBS & DISCOS

Gina – Il Bandito Nightly live music and shows. Loud and active.
 Piazzale Miramonti 10, Sauze d'Oulx  012 285 0671

Schuss Disco Dance till dawn at this hold-over from the original
disco era, still going loud and strong after 40 years.  Via Clotes 1,
Sauze d'Oulx  012 285 0194

Wine Bar Gran Trun Good wine list, nice environment and light food.
 Via Assietta 37, Sauze d'Oulx  012 285 0016

RESTAURANTS

Bardosteria £–££ Bardonecchia's best restaurant. The chef is vigilent about his use of locally produced organic ingredients, and dishes are hugely generous – the gigantic *Gran Plateau di Formaggi* is like a ploughman's lunch on steroids. ⓐ Via Medail 33, Bardonecchia ⓣ 012 299 862 ⓛ Daily

Du Grand Père ££ Set in a 17th-century house, this attractive restaurant serves well-prepared traditional fare. ⓐ Via Forte Seguin 14, Sestriere ⓣ 012 275 5970

Ristorante Bar Biovey ££ With well-prepared and ample servings, this chef-owned dining room is several cuts above the usual ski resort dining. ⓐ Via Generale Cantore (near the lower Jafferau lift station), Bardonecchia ⓣ 012 299 9215 ⓛ Wed–Mon, closed Tues

Restaurante Stazione ££ Sample Piemontese specialities, such as *arrosto al fieno Savoiardo* (meat roasted and infused with aromas of alpine flowers). ⓐ Corso Stati Uniti 4–6, Susa ⓣ 012 2262 2226

Il Cantun del Barbabuc ££–£££ Regional dishes using locally produced ingredients. The soups are especially good. ⓐ Via Luigi Faure 3, Sauze d'Oulx ⓣ 012 285 8593

Il Capricorno £££ Probably the best restaurant in town, and in winter they'll bring you here by snowmobile. ⓐ Via Case Sparse 21, Sauze d'Oulx ⓣ 012 285 0273 ⓦ www.chaletilcapricorno.it

ACCOMMODATION

Lodging options in this region vary from luxury hotels – especially in Sestriere – to village B&Bs and cosy chalets on mountainsides near ski lifts. In Sestriere, many hotels close in summer. Avoid August, unless you reserve early, when half of Turin empties into these same mountain resorts.

Hotel Napoleon £ The Napoleon is located in the centre of town and has been run by the Vanara family since 1970. A bit austere on the outside, it's attractive, bright and comfortable inside – and good value. ⓐ Via Mazzini 44, Susa ⓣ 012 262 2855 ⓕ 012 231900 ⓦ www.hotelnapoleon.it

La Posta £ The three rooms in this B&B are freshly renovated, with private baths, TVs and private entrances. ⓐ Via Nazionale, 15 Frazione La Ruà, Pragelato ⓣ/ⓕ 012 278 940 ⓦ www.lapostapragelato.it

Hotel Betulla £–££ Many of the 40 modern rooms in this chalet-style building, close to skiing, have balconies. ⓐ Viale della Vittoria 4, Bardonecchia ⓣ 012 299 9846 ⓕ 012 299 9104 ⓦ www.mediturhotels.it

Hotel Bucaneve £–££ Although a larger hotel, the public spaces are welcoming, and there's also a covered swimming pool. ⓐ Viale della Vecchia 2, Bardonecchia ⓣ 012 299 9892 ⓕ 012 299 9980 ⓦ www.hotelbucanevebardonecchia.it

THE VIA LATTEA

Literally the 'Milky Way', this system of ski trails covers the upper parts of the Susa and Chisone valleys and criss-crosses the border between Italy and France. The system encompasses more than 400 km (250 miles) of Alpine and Nordic trails with numerous cable cars, chairlifts and T-bars. Snow shoeing, iceskating, heli-skiing and snowmobiling are available within the system, and lodgings can be arranged so skiers need not return to a base every night. Ⓦ www.vialattea.it

Hotel Sciatori ££ The 25-room alpine chalet offers bed and breakfast, half- or full-board. ⓐ Via San Filippo 5, Borgata Sestriere Ⓣ 012 270 323 Ⓕ 012 270 196 Ⓦ www.hotelsciatorisestriere.it

Il Capricorno ££–£££ Modern and very comfortable, this seven-room inn is convenient for the Pian della Rocca chairlift. ⓐ Via Case Sparse 21, Sauze d'Oulx Ⓣ 012 285 0273 Ⓕ 012 285 0055 Ⓦ www.chaletilcapricorno.it

Grand Hotel Principi di Piemonte ££–£££ The modern hotel with fitness facilities and Turkish bath is close to the Via Lattea. ⓐ Via Sauze 3/B, Sestriere Ⓣ 012 27941 Ⓕ 012 275 5411 Ⓦ www.gh-principipiemonte.it

Gran Paradiso & the Val d'Aosta

Just north of Turin, at the boundary between the Piedmont and
Val d'Aosta regions, is Italy's oldest national park, the 70,010-hectare
(173,000-acre) Gran Paradiso. Like so many other of the region's treasures,
it was a legacy of the Savoys, who donated their 2,023-hectare
(5,000-acre) hunting reserve in 1919 as its nucleus. Beyond its
ever-white peaks is the richly historic Val d'Aosta, a major trade
and military route since the Celts, and Rome's northernmost
outpost two millennia ago. It's a land of castles (about 100 of them),
Roman remains, Gothic art, green meadows of wildflowers, crystal
lakes and world-class ski resorts.

SIGHTS & ATTRACTIONS

The very fact that it is at the foot of three of Europe's most famous
peaks – Mont Blanc, Monta Rosa and the Matterhorn – should make
the Val d'Aosta one of Italy's most visited regions, but the opposite is
true. Although the route down the narrow valley of the Dora Baltea
river was heavily travelled in antiquity – the Roman way-station at
Aosta grew to such splendour that Aosta was called the 'Rome of
the Alps' – today it is the playground of skiers and hikers, but not
many others. The old Roman road has been replaced by the S26 and
paralleled by the A5 autostrada, which affords stunning views as it
whisks cars from Turin to the Mont Blanc tunnel. Nothing is far from
these two roads, which will form the spine of your travel route.

Castles

The Dora Baltea's upper valley has an astonishing number of castles
for an area of its size. In various stages of repair, from over-restored

○ Val d'Aosta is watched over by the magnificent Mont Blanc

to crumbling, more than 80 of them once defended the valley from invaders or collected tolls from passing merchants and pilgrims. Today these provide a moody backdrop to little towns, plus good photo opportunities. Below Aosta are the fortifications that spill from hilltop Bard and the 15th-century Issogne Castle, a short walk from the Verrès train station. Aymavilles has a tiny turreted 14th-century castle, while Verrès is considered one of Europe's best examples of late Gothic military building. Some, including Fénis and Sarre, are restored or contain museums.

Cogne

Cogne sits at the end of a valley, with views of broad green meadows and a wall of white-topped mountains. On all sides are the rocky cliffs that characterise these Alpine peaks. Like many Val d'Aosta towns, bilingual Cogne seems as French as it is Italian. Even deeper into the mountains, at the end of the valley is tiny Lillaz, where Cascata di Lillaz drops in a series of long waterfalls, a short walk from the village. Hiking trails into the park begin here and from nearby Valnontry, where there is park information at Giardino Alpino Paradisia, an alpine garden

FUNIVIA DEL MONTE BIANCO (MONT BLANC CABLE CAR)

On a clear day, few experiences in Europe beat the cable-car trip 3,225 m (10,000 ft) up the mountain. It goes up to Punta Helbronner on the French border, before riding on, suspended over the glacier, to the ski resort of Chamonix, France.

The ride begins at La Palud, 4 km (2 miles) from Courmayeur.

ⓐ Entreves ⓞ 0165 846 658 ⓦ www.courmayeur-montblanc.com
ⓛ Early July–late Aug

with local plants labelled and described (ⓐ Giardino Alpino Paradisia
ⓣ 0165 741 47 ⓦ www.parks.it ⓛ June–Sept). A half-day hike leads
from the garden to the mountain *rifugio* (refuge) at Vittorio Sella,
passing the farmhouses of Herbetet and magnificent views of glaciers.
This is a trip for good weather only, as the path is quite open.

Courmayeur & Monte Bianco

Although it's right under Europe's mightiest piece of rock, Monte Bianco
(Mont Blanc), the actual mountain is hidden from view in Courmayeur
by a smaller, closer peak. But the scenery from its high (literally) street
is still good. The glamour is the town's main attraction, apart from its
location, although the Alpine Museum (see page 136) is worth a stop,
too. ⓐ Turismo Piazzale Monte Bianco 13, Courmayeur ⓣ 0165 842 060

Gran Paradiso National Park – north

Those interested in more than hiking should go to the park's
northern sector, reached from the A5 near Aosta. The few roads
that penetrate the park's wilderness follow valleys, ending at remote
villages and hamlets, most of which have seasonal visitors centres
that include small museums. From these villages, trails climb to
views of rocky peaks inhabited by elusive ibex and chamois.
ⓝ Hourly trains from Porta Susa to Aosta. Buses to valleys in the
park include SVAP (ⓣ 800 256 552 or 0165 411 25 ⓦ www.svap.it)
and SAVDA (ⓣ 0165 262 027 ⓦ www.savda.it)

Gran Paradiso National Park – south

No roads cross the wall formed by 4,061-m (12,590-ft) Mt Gran
Paradiso, rising at the border of Piedmont and Val d'Aosta regions.
Roads and tracks from the south lead to hiking trails and mountain
refuges; this southern part of the park will interest outdoors enthusiasts

and climbers, who can get information at the visitors centre in Noasca.
Tourist office ⓐ Segreteria turistica del Parco, Noasca, Valle Orco
ⓣ 0124 901 070

Monte Cervino (Matterhorn)

It is ironic that arguably the ugliest of all Alpine resorts sits in one of
the Alps' most beautiful locations. The Matterhorn, known to Italians
as Cervino, is even more dramatic from the Italian side than it is in
its iconic Swiss setting, but Zermatt has done far better by it. You
still need to go all the way to Breuil-Cervinia to board cable cars to
its upper slopes, but stop first at Lago Bleu, a few kilometres before
town. Its waters mirror the mountain, whose distinctive shape rises
straight ahead, framed in trees. Benches are provided for picnickers.
Tourist office ⓐ Via JA Carrel 29, Cervinia ⓣ 0166 949 136
ⓦ www.montecervino.it

Roman sites

Roman walls still encircle the Romans' Augusta Praetoria, now Aosta,
with guard towers still standing. But even more impressive are the
well-preserved Arch of Augustus and the Roman theatre, of which
an entire wall still stands almost 2,000 years later. Burrowing beneath
the city are catacombs; a map of Roman Aosta is free at the tourist
information office (where there is a 21st-century free internet point).
An archaeological museum (see page 136) helps paint the picture of the
city in Roman times. Tourist office ⓐ Piazza Chanoux 8 ⓣ 0165 236 627

Sant'Orso

Aosta's monastic complex just kept growing over the centuries and
is a catalogue of successive artistic styles, distributed among its church,
bell tower, cloister and crypts. The highlight is the cloister, with fine

stone carving on its columns. ❷ Via Sant'Orso, Aosta ❶ 0165 262 026
🕓 09.00–19.00 Tues–Sat, 12.00–19.00 Sun (summer); 09.30–12.00,
14.00–17.30 Mon–Sat, 14.00–17.30 Sun (winter)

CULTURE

No museum in the Val d'Aosta comes close to outshining
Turin's wealth of them, but several are of note to those with special
interests, and the restored Fénis Castle is worth a stop. Tourist office
❷ AIAT Castello di Sarre ❶ 0165 257 854 🅦 www.granparadiso.net
🕓 08.30–12.30, 14.00–18.00 Mon–Sat, 08.30–12.30 Sun, July & Aug;
08.30–12.30, 14.00–18.00 Mon, Tues & Thur–Sat, 08.30–12.30, Wed,
closed Sun, Dec–June

Castello di Fénis

The restored castle has a lovely 15th-century courtyard with a curved
stairway rising to wooden balconies. The courtyard and chapel are
painted in frescoes, most in excellent condition. ❷ Fénis ❶ 0165 764 263
🅦 www.comune.fenis.ao.it 🕓 09.00–19.00 mid-Mar–June & Sept,
09.00–20.00 July & Aug

Castello Reale

Built in 1710 on the foundations of a 13th-century fortified manor,
the castle became the hunting lodge of Italy's last king, Umberto,
and it was here that his wife, Princess Maria Jose, was sent with the
children after her unsuccessful attempt to secure a separate peace
between Italy and the USA during World War II. ❷ Sarre ❶ 0165 257 539
🕓 10.00–12.30, 13.30–17.30 Tues–Sat, 10.00–12.30, 13.30–18.00 Sun,
closed Mon. Admission charge

Museo Alpina Duca degli Abruzzi

The Alpine Guides Society of Courmayeur has restored their historic
Guides House to contain a museum of Alpine climbing and life.
Along with historical artefacts and memorabilia is an excellent
display of mountain photography. ⓐ Piazza Henry 2, Courmayeur
ⓣ 0165 842 064 ⓛ 09.30–18.30 Tues–Sun, closed Mon

Museo Archeologico

Despite its many Roman buildings, Aosta is not rich in Roman
treasures, but it has a good museum with artefacts from Neolithic
through medieval times. ⓐ Piazza Roncas 1, Aosta ⓣ 0165 275 902
ⓦ www.regione.vda.it ⓛ 09.00–19.00

Museo e canile dell'ospizio (Hospice Museum & Dog Museum)

At the top of the Gran San Bernardo Pass, 35km (22 miles) from Aosta,
is a showy panorama of snow-capped mountains. Just over the Swiss
border is a museum dedicated to the monk who built the first travellers'
hospice, after whom the pass and the breed of rescue dogs were
named. There's usually a couple of the dogs on-hand (but without
kegs, sadly). ⓣ (41) 27 787 1236 ⓛ 08.00–19.30, mid-June–mid-Oct

RETAIL THERAPY

With its abundance of forests, the Val d'Aosta is known for its fine
woodcarving. This takes the form of both traditional pieces and
thoroughly contemporary designs in kitchenware and household
décor. Cogne, in particular, is a centre, with several shops selling toys,
Christmas ornaments, kitchen utensils and decorative sculptures.
Courmayeur is the place to find the latest ski and sportswear as
well as trendy fashions. In Aosta, a wide variety of local products,

● *Just the place to shop for souvenirs of your stay – Cogne*

from wines and pasta to the famous local wildflower honey, are displayed in small shops and boutiques along Via San Ansalmo.

Da Mastro Geppetto Woodenware, decorations and toys by a master craftsman. ● Via Bougeois 1, Cogne ● 0165 749 156

IVAT Wrought-iron, baskets and woodcarving, in elegant contemporary and traditional styles. ● Rue Dr Grappein 32, Cogne ● 0165 743 22

Les Amis du Bois A cooperative shop owned by local master woodcarvers. ● Frazione Villes Dessus 9, Introd (16 km (10 miles) from Aosta) ● 0165 955 57

TAKING A BREAK

The mountain *rifugios* (refuges) offer hearty soups to skiers in winter and full meals for hikers in the summer. The tourist office in Aosta has a list of these, as do the park information offices. All the ski resort towns, as well as Aosta, have plenty of cafés.

Pizzeria du Tunnel £–££ Really good pizza is served at this popular rustic place. ⓐ Via Circonvallazione, Courmayeur ⓣ 0165 841 705

Pizzeria Trattoria Lou £–££ Hand-made pizza and traditional hearty mountain dishes. ⓐ Frazione Epinel 27b, Cogne ⓣ 0165 751 973 ⓛ 12.30–14.00, 19.30–22.00, closed Thur in off-season

Rifugio Vittorio Sella £–££ This *rifugio* is in the Lauson Valley, about two and a half hours' walk from the alpine garden, a good destination for a morning hike. ⓐ Frazione Valnontey, Cogne ⓣ 0165 743 10 ⓦ www.rifugiosella.com ⓛ 12.30–15.00, 19.15–21.00, late Mar–late Sept; closed late Sept–late Mar

AFTER DARK

Courmayeur's population of high-altitude high rollers brings nightlife – and prices to match – but if you've brought your trendiest sportswear (this season's, please) you can happily while away some time lounging in the cafés watching Fifi and Mimi parade past with their owners, on jewelled leashes. The upside of this pretty cluster of jetset habitats is that the restaurants are very good. While nightlife exists, Courmayeur is not exactly the best resort for party animals. At most of the ski resort towns, the action is in the *après-ski* hours. Expect bars with the classiest clientele – such as Courmayeur's Cadran Solaire and Bar Roma – to have ritzier prices, but at least they lay on free snacks. Cheese fondue is a favourite après-ski dish.

RESTAURANTS

La Cave de Tillier Ristorante Brasserie £–££ Tender potato gnocchi in creamy fontina cheese sauce is the house speciality first course at this cheery steakhouse. ➋ Via de Tillier 40, Aosta ➊ 0165 230 133

Osteria Trattoria Cretaz £–££ Local ingredients, such as venison with blueberries, distinguish this homey *osteria*. ➋ Frazione Cretaz, Cogne ➊ 0165 746 51 ➌ 12.00–14.00, 19.00–21.30, closed Wed in low season

Ristorante Praetoria £–££ Polenta is a local speciality, served here with rabbit. ➋ Via San Anselmo 9 ➊ 0165 443 56

La Clusaz Locanda Ristorante £££ Extraordinary cuisine, based on seasonal ingredients, served *prix fixe*. Starter options include their own cured meats. ➋ Gignod (SS27 on the way to the Gran San Bernardo pass) ➊ 0165 560 75 ➍ www.laclusaz.it ➎ Daily (closed lunch Tues & Wed)

CLUBS, BARS & DISCOS

Fashion Café DJ music until all hours, with a lively and friendly crowd. ➋ Località Amérique 17, Aosta ➊ 349 555 4694 ➍ www.fashioncafeaosta.com ➌ 23.00–05.00 Fri & Sat, closed Sun–Thur

Planet Disco Bar Late-night option with a DJ, which is not a good choice if you plan on first tracks in the morning. ➋ Centro Sportivo, Plan des Lizzes, Courmayeur ➊ 0165 844 409

ACCOMMODATION

Lodgings in the Val d'Aosta range from rustic mountain *rifugios*, or hikers' dorms, to beautiful and luxurious grand hotels. In between these are modest *alberghi* and charming *locande*, often owned by a talented chef whose dining room makes the *locanda* a real destination. As you might expect, the upper-end hotels cluster in classier resorts like Courmayeur.

Rifugio Vittorio Sella £ The *rifugio*, which sleeps 160 hikers, was once a hunting lodge of King Vittorio Emanuele II. It is about two and a half hours' walk from the alpine garden. ⓐ Frazione Valnontey, Cogne ⓣ 0165 743 10 ⓦ www.rifugiosella.com ⓛ Late Mar–late Sept

Bellevue ££–£££ The view from here is superb, overlooking the green (or white) valley with mountains all around. Good restaurant and an indoor swimming pool. ⓐ Rue Grand Paradis 22, Cogne ⓣ 0165 748 25 ⓦ www.hotelbellevue.it

Hotel Europe ££–£££ Modern hotel in the historic centre, a few steps from the main piazza and Roman sites and a short walk from the train station. Covered parking, free internet access and welcoming staff. ⓐ Piazza Narbonne 8, Aosta ⓣ 0165 236 363 ⓦ www.ethotels.com

Romantik Hotel Villa Novecento £££ Luxuriously appointed and individually decorated rooms in a restored mansion, with sauna, whirlpool tubs and fitness centre. ⓐ Viale Monte Bianco 64, Courmayeur ⓣ 0165 843 000 ⓦ www.villanovecento.it

ⓞ *The rack railway to Basilica di Superga*

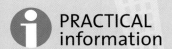

PRACTICAL
information

Directory

GETTING THERE

Turin's location in northern Italy, close to Milan, makes it easily accessible from anywhere in Europe – or the world. Depending on where you begin, the options include air, rail, bus and car, or a combination.

By air

If you're coming from the UK and Europe, **Ryanair** (ⓦ www.ryanair.com) flies daily from Stansted to Turin's Sandro Pertini (Caselle) Airport, often at incredibly low fares. **EasyJet** (ⓦ www.easyjet.com) serves Turin directly from Luton and **British Airways** (ⓦ www.britishairways.com) has daily flights direct to Turin from Gatwick. Additionally, most major airports offer flights to Turin via national carriers. Connections are also possible via Milan and Genoa. Milan Malpensa has a direct bus to Turin (see page 46) and Genoa is just under two hours by train. There are no direct flights to Turin from the USA or Canada, but several airlines fly from major US gateways to Milan's Malpensa Airport, connected to Turin by direct shuttle bus or by an easy train connection via Milan's Stazione Centrale (ⓦ www.ferroviedellostato.it).

There are no direct flights offered to any Italian city from Australia or New Zealand, so the best plan is to book the best price to a major European hub, with an onward connection to Turin or Milan.

Although there are fewer ready-made packages to Turin than to resort holiday destinations, you can sometimes combine air fare, lodging and car hire into a money-saving package. Ask about the possibilities when booking flights. It's always wise to secure your trip with travel insurance: most tour operators offer insurance options, or you can insure the trip independently to protect your investment.

Many people are aware that air travel emits CO_2, which contributes to climate change. You may be interested in the possibility of lessening the environmental impact of your flight through Climate Care, which offsets your CO_2 by funding environmental projects around the world. Visit Ⓦ www.climatecare.org

By road

The Mont Blanc Tunnel speeds the trip across the Alps into the Piedmont along the A5 autostrada. The other major route across the Alps is from Lyon, through Chambéry, France, via the Traforo del Frejus tunnel. Driving time from Lyon or Zurich takes about four hours. Italy, like the rest of the continent, drives on the right-hand side of the road.

Although the journey is certainly time-consuming, one of the cheapest ways to travel to Turin from the UK is by bus, about 24 hours from London's Victoria Coach Station (☎ 0870 580 8080 Ⓦ www.nationalexpress.com).

By rail

With the arrival of Eurostar Italia services, Turin's Porta Susa station is now a direct link between Geneva and Milan, so a rail trip from London's Waterloo to Turin takes just over 11 hours. Less pricey are conventional trains connecting from Milan, Genoa or Lyon. Turin is on the main line from Paris to Milan. Travel time is 4 hours from Paris by Eurocity service, 6 hours by slower train, and 1 hour 40 minutes from Milan. Italian trains normally run on time (Ⓦ www.ferroviedellostato.it). Be sure to stamp your ticket with the date in one of the yellow machines on the platform of the station before boarding.

Travellers from outside Europe who plan to use trains should investigate the various multi-day train passes on Trenitalia and multi-country travel offered by **Rail Europe** (Ⓦ www.raileurope.com).

For travellers anywhere, Rail Europe offers a one-stop source of information, reservations and tickets.

Order the monthly *Thomas Cook European Rail Timetable* for up-to-date schedules of European international and national train services ❶ 01733 416477 Ⓦ www.thomascookpublishing.com

ENTRY FORMALITIES
Visa requirements

UK citizens with a valid passport may stay without a visa for an unlimited period. Citizens of the Republic of Ireland, USA, Canada,

⬤ *Turin is easily accessible by Eurostar from most major European cities*

New Zealand, Australia, Singapore and Israel need only a valid passport to enter Italy and do not require visas for stays of up to 90 days. Citizens of South Africa must have visas to enter Italy.

Customs

EU citizens can bring goods for personal use when arriving from another EU country, but must observe the limits on tobacco (800 cigarettes) and spirits (10 litres over 22 per cent alcohol, 90 litres of wine). Limits for non-EU nationals are 200 cigarettes and one litre of spirits, two of wine.

MONEY

The euro (€) is the official currency in Italy. €1 = 100 cents. It comes in notes of €5, €10, €20, €50, €100, €200 and €500. Coins are in denominations of €1 and €2, and 1, 2, 5, 10, 20 and 50 cents.

Currency exchange facilities and ATMs are near the arrival gates at both Caselle and Malpensa airports.

Avoid carrying large amounts of cash, and if you must, hide it well in several concealed pockets and security pouches. Safer are travellers' cheques, which are accepted at banks, major hotels and by larger stores, but difficult to cash elsewhere. If possible, bring at least one major credit card; Visa is the most commonly accepted. Most small hotels, *agriturismo* properties and small restaurants do not accept cards.

Best for obtaining euros are credit or debit cards. ATMs (*bancomat*) offer the best exchange rates, are found even in small towns and never close. Ask your card issuer before leaving home what network you can use in Italy and make sure that your PIN number can be used abroad. Banks are usually open from Monday to Friday 08.30–13.00 or 13.30, with an additional hour mid-afternoon, usually some time between 14.45 and 16.30. Try to have enough euros to last over weekends, when banks close and ATMs may be out of money or out of order. Try to arrive with euros, especially on a weekend.

HEALTH, SAFETY & CRIME

While you need to be aware of your surroundings in any city, and avoid walking alone at night and in seedy neighbourhoods, Turin is not particularly dangerous for travellers. Guard against pickpockets by carrying (well hidden) only the cash you need. Waist packs and bum bags label you as a tourist and make you a particular target anywhere. Be especially wary of crowded areas, such as train stations, buses and street markets, and avoid groups of small children who try to engage you in conversation. They are fast and work expertly in teams. Keep cameras firmly in your hand and the strap around your neck (or better yet, hidden away). Never leave cameras or handbags slung over the back of your chair. Overall, however, petty theft is not especially common in Turin.

Report any thefts immediately, and be sure to get a copy of the *denuncia* (report) for insurance. Police are of two varieties, the carabinieri, or national police, and the *vigili*, or local officers. Both are armed and can make arrests, but the *vigili* are usually more concerned with traffic and parking. You can report a crime to either, but the paperwork must be completed at a *questura* (police station).

Drinking water is safe in Turin, as is food; it is wise to carry your favourite medication for upset stomach, since travellers anywhere are more likely to eat and drink things their systems are unaccustomed to. Should you become ill or have an accident, medical care is quite good and free to EU residents who carry a European Health Insurance Card (EHIC). Non-EU residents should carry travellers health insurance if their own coverage does not cover re-imbursement, and should also consider emergency medical evacuation insurance. Emergency treatment at hospitals is free to everyone. For police and medical emergency numbers, see Emergencies, page 154).

As a pedestrian, always look both ways when crossing even on one-way streets, since bus lanes sometimes travel in the opposite direction. Those from left-hand drive countries need to be especially careful because traffic will be approaching from an unfamiliar direction. There are fewer motorised two-wheeled vehicles here than in most Italian cities, but you should always be aware of these approaching between vehicles or emerging suddenly from alleyways.

OPENING HOURS

Major attractions open 08.30 or 09.00 to 19.00 or 19.30 with Monday closing. Smaller ones may have shorter hours and close for lunch. Hours are subject to change, so ask at the tourist office for the most up-to-date times (websites are notoriously out of date).

Banks open Mon–Fri 08.30–13.00 or 13.30, with an additional hour mid-afternoon. Shops generally open 09.00 or 10.00 until 19.00 or 19.30 Mon–Sat, and sometimes close for an hour or two at lunch and/or Monday mornings. Sunday opening is becoming more common.

Street markets open about 07.00 and close around midday. Most pharmacies are open Mon–Sat 08.00–13.00 and 16.00–20.00, and a sign on the door will direct you to the nearest one open Sundays and nights.

TOILETS

Public buildings, such as museums, generally have clean toilets in the publicly accessible areas near the entrance (or will let you in to use one if you look desperate), and you will find occasional public facilities in the centre of the city (Piazza Solferino's is in the Atrium).

But the fastest and easiest solution is to step into a bar or café and go directly to the back, following the sign 'toilet' or 'WC' or the universal symbols. These may not be entirely savoury affairs (always carry your own paper), but they are available. At public toilets, be prepared to pay a small fee, usually €0.50.

⬥ *Cycling Turin's kilometres of bicycle paths is fun for all ages*

CHILDREN

Italians love children – and spoil them – but in Turin they rarely take them out to dinner in the evening, especially to classier restaurants. As a result, these types of places will not have appropriate chairs or children's portions and the staff may relegate you to a corner near the kitchen. Better to choose a small neighbourhood *trattoria*, where your whole family will be welcomed. Hotels can usually provide cots with advance notice, and you will rarely be charged for a child staying in a room with adults. Special infant needs, such as baby food and nappies, are available in supermarkets, but for a shorter stay it's easier to bring familiar brands from home.

Turin has a number of child-friendly sights and activities on offer. Rides appealing to children include noisy, lumbering trams (children under 1 m/3 ft tall ride free), the Mole's glass elevator (see page 100) and the rack railway climbing to Superga, across the river (see page 99). Borgo Medievale (see page 96) is a low-key, free mock-medieval village, complete with an armour shop, and frequent hands-on activities for children (ask if any are scheduled that day).

Older children will appreciate the mummies and other Egyptian relics in the Egyptian Museum (see page 62) and the creepy tunnels of the Museo Pietro Micca (see pages 81–2). In addition to the elevator in the Mole, that building houses the excellent cinema museum, with sets and props from famous films, plus animation exhibits.

Across the river, the abandoned zoo becomes Experimenta in summer, a science experience centre with plenty of activities for all ages. ⓐ Corso Casale 15 ⓞ 800 329 329 ⓦ www.experimenta.to.it ⓛ 16.00–24.00 Mon–Fri, 15.00–24.00 Sat, 10.00–22.00 Sun, June–Sept; 15.00–20.00 Tues–Sat, 10.00–22.00 Sun, closed Mon, late Sept–early Nov; 15.00–20.00 Sat, 10.00–22.00 Sun, Nov; closed Dec–May ⓝ Bus/Tram: 3, 30, 61, 66, 75. Admission charge

COMMUNICATIONS

Internet

Internet access is increasingly available, both in hotels and internet points and cafés around the city. Most upper-end hotels have in-room access (Wi-Fi is becoming more prevalent). In addition to the following internet wine bar, tourist information office and kiosks can provide lists of internet cafés and public access points such as libraries.

Il Bu.net ⓐ Via San Quintino 13/F ⓣ 011 440 7517 ⓦ www.il-bu.net

Phone

All Turin numbers begin with 011, which must be dialled from inside or outside the city. Numbers vary between eight and nine digits, with a few shorter ones remaining. Numbers beginning with 800 are toll-free. To use public telephones, buy a *scheda telefonica* (telephone card) from a *tabacchio*, designated by a white 'T' on a dark background. Hotel telephones usually carry a high surcharge, but not always, so ask at the desk.

Mobile phone numbers begin with 3; if you see an old number with the prefix 03, omit the zero. UK, New Zealand and Australian mobile phones will work in Italy; many US and Canadian cell phones may not. Check with your service provider before travelling.

Post

Despite what you may have heard, the Italian postal service is quite reliable. For letters and postcards you can buy stamps at any *tabacchio*, and for special services you can go to a post office at Via Alfieri 10 in central Turin or at Via Nizza 10, behind Porta Nuova station. If you pay extra for *prioritaria*, your card or letter should arrive the next day in Italy, within three days in the UK and about five days elsewhere. Rates change often, so check at the *tabacchio* selling the stamps.

TELEPHONING ABROAD
To make an international call, dial 00, then the country code (UK 44, Republic of Ireland 353, US and Canada 1, Australia 61, New Zealand 64, South Africa 27) and number, omitting the initial zero in UK numbers.

TELEPHONING ITALY
To call Turin from outside Italy, dial the international access code (00 in the UK and Ireland, 011 in the US), then Italy's country code of 39, then the number (which will be prefixed with 011 for Turin).

ELECTRICITY

Electrical appliances used in the UK will work in Italy with an adapter, but those from the US and Canada will need a transformer to convert from 110v to 220v. Plugs are two- or three-pin, round pin types.

TRAVELLERS WITH DISABILITIES

The building boom for the Olympics has helped improve facilities for the disabled in Turin, since new buildings must meet the new standards for wheelchair access. While the law does require Turin restaurants to have both tables and toilets accessible to wheelchairs, in practice most do not. A good bet are the restaurants in modern buildings, such as the Lingotto and those in hotels. A call in advance can determine what is available. Major sights with ramped access, lifts and suitable toilets include the Egyptian and cinema museums, GAM (the modern art museum), the Agnelli gallery in the Lingotto complex and Rivoli Palace. Turismo Torino, in the Atrium – itself wheelchair accessible – can provide current lists.

The entire bus system is being upgraded to include access for the disabled, and some tram lines (4 and 10 among them) are already fitted. Some cars on trains from the airport have wheelchair access. Most trains have access, but you must reserve at least 24 hours in advance and go about an hour early to fill in forms. Each station (in theory) has an *Ufficio Disabili* and many have specially outfitted waiting rooms for wheelchair passengers.

Call a taxi ahead to be sure of having one with space for a folded wheelchair, or call the special taxi service for those with disabilities (☎ 011 581 16). Most public toilets have special wheelchair facilities.

For current information before leaving home, contact **RADAR** (ⓐ 12 City Forum, 250 City Rd, London EC1V 8AF ☎ (020) 7250 0212 ⓦ www.radar.org.uk).

TOURIST INFORMATION
Tourist offices
Turismo Torino ☎ 011 535 181 🖷 011 530 070 ⓦ www.turismotorino.org

Information points
Atrium Torino ⓐ Piazza Solferino 🕐 09.30–19.00
Information Turismo ⓐ Porta Nuova railway station 🕐 09.30–19.30.
Information Turismo ⓐ Caselle Airport 🕐 08.00–23.00

Useful websites
ⓦ **www.turismotorino.org** The official and very useful site of Turismo Torino, with extensive listings of attractions, dining, entertainment and other information.
ⓦ **www.extratorino.it** Another excellent and easy-to-navigate site with useful details on attractions, dining, shopping and more.
ⓦ **www.piemondo.it** Information on the entire Piedmont region,

with useful links and information on lodging and travel.

ⓦ **www.enit.it** The site of the Italian Government Tourist Board (Ente Nazionale Italiano per il Turismo, or ENIT), with general information on travel in Italy, as well as regional coverage.

BACKGROUND READING

Whether in preparation for your trip, or at your leisure while in the city, there are plenty of books that will immerse you in Turin's culture and history. For aspiring detectives, try Michael Dibdin's *A Long Finish*, featuring Aurelio Zen, an Italian Criminalpol inspector, or Carlo Fruttero & Franco Lucentini's *The Sunday Woman (La donna della domenica)*, winner of the Italian 'Book of the Year' prize in 1973. Sort the Shroud of Turin's facts from fiction with Brendan Whiting's *The Shroud Story*. History buffs should delve into the Agnelli family's turbulent history, with *Agnelli Fiat and the Network of Italian Power*, by Alan Friedman, and foodies can pick up a copy of Carlo Petrini's 2007 book, *Slow Food Nation*. And finally, Primo Levi, a Turin native, wrote his internationally acclaimed *If This is a Man*, upon his return to Turin after World War II, along with collections of poems and many of his other classics.

TRAVEL INSURANCE

EU citizens are covered for emergency health care in Italy – be sure to take along your European Health Insurance Card (EHIC). However, this European agreement tends to reimburse only the direst of medical situations. Wherever you are from, ensure that you take out adequate travel insurance to cover any emergency (theft, lost luggage, etc.) that could occur on your trip.

Emergencies

In an emergency, dial the following:

Ambulance/emergency medical care ❶ 118
Fire ❶ 115
Police ❶ 112

MEDICAL SERVICES

There are several sources of information on English-speaking doctors.
Ask your consulate for a list, or go prepared with the directory published
by the International Association for Medical Assistance to Travellers
(IAMAT), a non-profit organisation that provides medical information
on health-related travel issues all over the world, as well as a list of
English-speaking doctors (ⓦ www.iamat.org).

Hospital accident and emergency departments, (ask for the
pronto soccorso) are open 24 hours daily, and must treat you free
of charge in an emergency. Several hospitals are grouped in Turin's
Lingotto neighbourhood, some with specialities.

Azienda Sanitaria Ospedaliera San Giovanni Battista ⓐ Corso
Bramante 88/90 ❶ 011 633 1633, Pronto Soccorso 011 633 5248
Ⓝ Bus/Tram: 1, 17, 18, 34, 42, 45, 47, 66

Ospedale Maria Vittoria ⓐ Via Cibrario 72, Pronto Soccorso Corso
Tassoni, 46 ❶ 011 439 3111 Ⓝ Bus/Tram: 9, 13, 16, 29, 59, 71

POLICE

To report a theft, missing person or any other serious matter,
go to the *questura*, or police station, not far from Porta Susa station.
If insurance is involved, ask for a *denuncia*, a stamped form that you
must have for filing claims.

Questura ⓐ Corso Vinzaglio 10 ❶ 011 558 81

EMERGENCY PHRASES

Help!
Aiuto!
Ahyootoh!

Fire!
Fuoco!
Fwohkoh!

Stop!
Fermi!
Fehrmee!

Call an ambulance/a doctor/the police/the fire service!
Chiami un'ambulanza/un medico/la polizia/i pompieri!
Kyamee oon ahmboolahntsa/oon mehdeecoh/
lah pohleetseeyah/ee pohmpyehree!

EMBASSIES & CONSULATES

American Consulate General ⓐ Via Principe Amedeo 2/10,
20121 Milano ⓣ 02 290 351 ⓕ 02 2900 1165
ⓦ http://milan.usconsulate.gov

Australian Consulate General ⓐ 3rd Floor, Via Borgogna 2,
20122 Milano ⓣ 02 777 041 ⓕ 02 777 04242
ⓦ www.italy.embassy.gov.au

British Consulate General ⓐ Via S Paolo 7, 20121 Milano
ⓣ 02 723 001, After office hours (emergency only) 335 810 6857
ⓕ 02 864 65081 ⓦ www.britishembassy.gov.uk/italy

Canadian Embassy ⓐ Via Zara 30, 00198 Roma ⓣ 06 854 443 937,
Emergency 06 854441 ⓦ www.canada.it

New Zealand Consulate General ⓐ Via Guido d'Arezzo 6,
20145 Milano ⓣ 02 499 0201 ⓕ 02 4801 2577
ⓦ www.nzembassy.com

South African Consulate General ⓐ Vicolo S.Giovanni sul Muro 4,
20121 Milano ⓣ 02 885 8581 ⓕ 02 8858 5848 ⓦ www.sudafrica.it

INDEX

A

accommodation 32–7,
    see also hotels
Agnelli family 18, 106–7
air connections 46, 142–3
airports 46
Aosta 130–40
Armeria Reale
    (Royal Amoury) 62
art nouveau 82
Aymavilles 132

B

banks 145–6
Bard 132
Bardonecchia 120
Basilica di Superga 94–6
Biblioteca Reale
    (Royal Library) 56
bicerin 88
boat trips 102
Borgo Medievale 96
bus connections 47, 143

C

cafés 66–8, 86–9, 108–10,
    125–6
Cappella della Pia
    Congregazione
    dei Banchieri
    e dei Mercanti 74
car hire 54
Castello del Valentino 96
Castello della Mandria 97
Castello di Fénis 135
Castello di Rivoli 97–98
Castello Reale, Sarre 135
Cathedral 76–7
Cesana Torinese 120
children 149
Cinema Museum 105
Cittadella 72–93
climate 8
clubs, bars & discos 28–9,
    71, 93, 114, 126, 139

Cogne 132–3, 136
Consolata, La 80
Corpus Domini
    church 74–6
Courmayeur 133, 136
credit cards 145
Cremagliera, La 99
culture 18–20
currency 145
customs regulations 145
cycling 31

D

disabilities,
    travellers with 151–2
driving 47, 143
Duomo di San Giovanni
    Battista 76–7

E

Egyptian Museum 62
electricity 151
embassies
    & consulates 155
emergencies 154–5
entertainment 28–9
events 8–11

F

Fénis 135
festivals 8–11, 43
food & drink 24–7
football 30
Forte di Exilles 123

G

Galleria Civica
    d'Arte Moderna
    e Contemporanea
    (GAM) 81
Galleria Sabauda 63
gay movement 17
Giardini Reali
    (Royal Gardens) 58
Gran Paradiso 130–40
Gran Paradiso National
    Park 133–4

H

health 146–7, 154
history 14–15
Holy Shroud of Turin 76, 83
hotels
    Alpine areas 128–9
    Turin 32–7
    Val d'Aosta 140

I

internet cafés 150

L

lifestyle 16–17
Lingotto complex, 30, 99

M

Matterhorn 134
Mole Antonelliana 100
money 145–6
Monte Bianco 132–3
Monte Cervino
    (Matterhorn) 134
Mountain Museum 105
Murazzi 100
Museo Alpina
    Duca degli Abruzzi,
    Courmayeur 136
Museo Archeologico,
    Aosta 136
Museo Civico
    Pietro Micca 81–2
Museo d'Arte Preistorica,
    Pinerolo 124
Museo del Costume delle
    Tradizioni delle Genti
    Alpine, Pragelato 125
Museo dell'Automobile
    104–5
Museo della Marionetta
    Piemontese 83
Museo della Sindone
    (Museum of the
    Holy Shroud) 83
Museo di Antichità 83–4
Museo Egizio 62

Museo Civico Etnografico,
  Bardonecchia 124
Museo Nazionale
  del Cinema 105
Museo Nazionale
  del Risorgimento
  Italiano 62–3
Museo Nazionale
  della Montagna 105
music 28–9, 113

N
nightlife 28–9

O
Olympics 116
opening hours 147
orientation 48–9
Orto Botanico 100–2

P
Palazzina di Caccia
  di Stupinigi 98
Palazzo Carignano 58–9
Palazzo Falletti
  di Barolo 77
Palazzo Madama 59
Palazzo Reale
  (Royal Palace) 63–4
Parco Naturale della
  Val Troncea 120–1
Parco Regionale
  La Mandria 97
Parco del Valentino 102
parking 47
passports & visas 144–5
phones 150
Piazza Castello 60–1
Piazza Consolata 77–8
Piazza San Carlo 61
Piazza Solferino 79
Piazza Vittorio Veneto 102
Pinacoteca Agnelli 106–7
Po, River 94
police 154
Porta Palatina 79

post 150
Pragelato 121
public holidays 11
public transport 49–54

Q
Quadrilatero 72–93

R
rail connections 47–8,
  143–4
Reggia di Venaria Reale 98
restaurants 26–7, 127, 138–9
Risorgimento 15, 62–3
riverside area,
  Turin 94–114
road connections 143
Rocca Medievale 103
Roman remains 79, 134
Royal Armoury 62
Royal Library 56
Royal Palace 56, 63–4
royal palaces 97–8

S
Sacra di San Michele 121
safety 48, 146–7
San Lorenzo church 58
San Massimo
  church 96–99
Sant'Orso 134–5
Santuario di Santa
  Maria Consolatrice 80
Sauze d'Oulx 121–2
Savoy centre 56–71
Savoy, House of 14, 18
seasons 8
Sestriere 122
shopping 22–3, 64–5,
  84–6, 107–8, 125, 136–7
skiing *see* winter sports
slow food 10, 12–13, 24, 112
sport 30–1
Susa 122

T
taxis 54
Teatro Regio 64
Teatro Romano 80
theatres 70–1, 92, 113–14
time difference 46
tipping 26–7
toilets 147–8
Torino Card 52
tourist information 152–3
Turin Shroud 76, 83

V
Val d'Aosta 130–40
Val del Chisone 123
Verrès 132
Via Garibaldi 72
Via Lattea ski trails 129
Via Po 61

W
weather 8
wine 25
wine bars 42–3
winter sports 30, 116–7

WHAT'S IN YOUR GUIDEBOOK?

Independent authors Impartial up-to-date information from our travel experts who meticulously source local knowledge.

Experience Thomas Cook's 165 years in the travel industry and guidebook publishing enriches every word with expertise you can trust.

Travel know-how Contributions by thousands of staff around the globe, each one living and breathing travel.

Editors Travel-publishing professionals, pulling everything together to craft a perfect blend of words, pictures, maps and design.

You, the traveller We deliver a practical, no-nonsense approach to information, geared to how you really use it.

Editorial/project management: Lisa Plumridge
Copy editor: Lesley McCave
Layout: Alison Rayner
Proofreader: Wendy Janes

continued on page 160

SPOT A CITY IN SECONDS

This great range of pocket city guides will have you in the know in no time. Lightweight and packed with detail on the most important things from shopping and sights to non-stop nightlife, they knock spots off chunkier, clunkier versions. Titles include:

Amsterdam	Bratislava	Glasgow	Madrid	Salzburg
Antwerp	Bruges	Gothenburg	Marrakech	Sarajevo
Athens	Brussels	Granada	Milan	Seville
Barcelona	Bucharest	Hamburg	Monte Carlo	Sofia
Belfast	Budapest	Hanover	Munich	Stockholm
Belgrade	Cardiff	Helsinki	Naples	Strasbourg
Berlin	Cologne	Hong Kong	New York	St Petersburg
Bilbao	Copenhagen	Istanbul	Nice	Tallinn
Bologna	Cork	Kiev	Oslo	Toulouse
	Dubai	Krakow	Palermo	Turin
	Dublin	Leipzig	Palma	Valencia
	Dubrovnik	Lille	Paris	Venice
	Düsseldorf	Lisbon	Prague	Verona
	Edinburgh	Ljubljana	Porto	Vienna
	Florence	London	Reykjavik	Vilnius
	Frankfurt	Lyon	Riga	Warsaw
	Gdansk		Rome	Zagreb
	Geneva			Zurich
	Genoa			

The publishers would like to thank the following individuals and organisations for supplying their copyright photographs for this book: Fabrizio Argonauta, page 31; Adriano Bacchella, page 87; Roberto Caucino, page 5; Luca Chiartano, page 115; EPAT, page 91; Davide Fiorenzo De Conti, page 103; Guido Gobino, page 124; Kobayashi Hirofumi ©istockphoto.com, page 109; Martini & Rossi, page 16; Michele d'Ottavio, page 26; Claudio Penna, page 148; Marco Prandina ©istockphoto.com, page 21; Slow Food Archives, page 13; Stockxpert.com, page 144; Artem Svystun, page 116–7; Turismo Turino: pages 45, 55, (Veronica Rossi); 7 (Michele d'Ottavio); 19 (Museo Nazionale del Cinema); 85 (Giuseppe Bressi); 106 (Regione Piemonte); 70, 141; Stillman Rogers Photography, all other images.

Send your thoughts to
books@thomascook.com

- **Found a great bar, club, shop or must-see sight that we don't feature?**
- **Like to tip us off about any information that needs a little updating?**
- **Want to tell us what you love about this handy little guidebook and more importantly how we can make it even handier?**

Then here's your chance to tell all! Send us ideas, discoveries and recommendations today and then look out for your valuable input in the next edition of this title.

Email the above address (stating the title) or write to:
CitySpots Project Editor, Thomas Cook Publishing, PO Box 227, Coningsby Road, Peterborough PE3 8SB, UK.